Dried Up

Leaves

Shalara Wells

Table of Contents

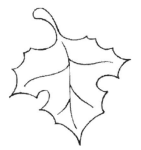

Fall

Imagine if bears didn't prepare for hibernation. What would become of them? Change is inevitable, but are we prepared for it? Our lives depend on preparation. So often we lose our battles because we are not prepared. The leaves dry up and fall away. The wind blows a little heavier. We must seize each moment because seasons come and go.

Chapter 1

Our lives are centered around seasons. The Bible says in Ecclesiastes 3:1-8, "To everything there is a season, and a time to every purpose under the heaven: A time to be born, and a time to die; a time to plant, and a time to pluck up that which is planted; A time to kill, and a time to heal; a time to break down, and a time to build up; A time to weep, and a time to laugh; a time to mourn, and a time to dance; A time to cast away stones, and a time to gather stones together; a time to embrace, and a time to refrain from embracing; A time to get, and a time to lose; a time to keep, and a time to cast away; A time to rend, and a time to sew; a time to keep silence, and a time to speak; A time to love, and a time to hate; a time of war, and a time of peace." I believe that it is, indeed, my season to heal and speak. We all go through things in life that shape and mold us into the people we are today. It's like the only way our hearts can be healed is if we unlock the padlock that's on our hearts. We create a closet in our hearts that we throw things into, put a padlock on it and we consider ourselves healed. The numbers to the combination are traumatic experiences that we've faced throughout our journey. It only takes courage for you to attempt to unlock it, but then you'll have to relive those horrific moments and sort them out. Fall is my favorite season. Not only was I born in October, but the weather is so beautiful. The colors of the leaves are beautiful. The reds, oranges and yellows create such beauty, and the wind is blowing just right.

As a child, we had this big magnolia tree in our backyard. The leaves were huge. I would take those leaves and crumble them in my hands and watch the wind take it away. I often wished I was those leaves, so that the wind would take me far, far away. I shouldn't have felt that way at the age of 5, but life has a funny way of weighing down on you, no matter what age you are. I know you're probably wondering why. What could be weighing on a 5-year-old so heavily? I'll start from the beginning. My beautiful mother gave birth to me at the very tender age of 14. Yes, that's right. She was only 14 years old. She told me how scared she was, and I could only imagine. She told me that my grandmother was so embarrassed that she stopped speaking to her until the halfway mark of her pregnancy. I guess once it sunk in and there was nothing she could do about it, she had no choice but to embrace it. My mom said she was so determined to get me out of her belly. The projects that we lived in is called Cedar Hill Circle, also known as "The Hill". The apartments literally made a circle. She said when it was close to her due date, she walked that circle so many times to force herself into labor. On October 16, 1989, her wish was granted. Her water finally broke. I was born with serious complications. Weighing 3 pounds with blood clots, I had to stay in the hospital for a few months, but of course, my mother and grandmother were there every chance they got. My mom said my Grandma Lynn fell in love with me the moment she laid eyes on me. I could tell by how much she spoiled me, as I got old enough to remember. Here we are living in the projects with my Grandma Lynn, my Grandpa Larry, my aunt and my uncle. We lived in a 3-bedroom apartment, but there was so much love there. They called me Nunny Bird because I was messy. I told on everybody, and I repeated everything I heard. I was the new annoying baby sister. Being that my mother had me at such a young age, my grandmother stepped in as mother figure up until my mother made 17 and got pregnant again. This time, unlike my father, this man wanted to be a family with us and wanted to marry her. My family was so happy for my mom. He moved us out of the projects into this pretty green and white house on St. John Street. The backyard was huge and there was that big magnolia tree I mentioned earlier. He brought me every doll and dollhouse I could ever dream of having. We had chickens and dogs. And for Easter, he would get us baby chicks and spray paint them pastel colors. My happiest day was when my baby sister was born. Allison Renee! She was so chunky and cute. She would stick her tongue out of her mouth when she smiled. It was the cutest thing ever. I finally had my very own little best friend. Everything was great, except for my mom thinking she was a beautician. I already didn't have a lot of hair and every time she hot combed my hair; she burned my ears. Don't laugh! Ok you can laugh, but it wasn't funny when the school called child protection services on her. The natural hair epidemic should've hit when I was growing up. I would've fit right in. We thought straight hair was good hair. Luckily, she didn't get in trouble.

Now I'm getting to a place where I must turn the combination on my padlock. I'm 5 years old. Thanksgiving breaks were always my favorite. Not only for the food, but for the time with family. My aunts, uncle and my great grandmother from New Orleans would come visit with all their children. We would all be jam packed in that little apartment on "The Hill". During this particular break, my stepdad said we couldn't sleep over. We had to come home. My mom worked nights at a nursing home, and my stepdad worked days. He picked us up from my grandmother's at about 6pm and got us home and ready for bed. I laid in bed and planned my whole day for the next day. I was going to play jump rope with my cousins and ride my bike I got last Christmas, play hopscotch and do all kind of cool stuff. I finally fell asleep, but I felt something rubbing against my leg. As I opened my eyes, I saw it was my stepfather. He put his finger over his lips saying, "Shhhh", but I was confused about what was about to take place. He pulled my underwear down and began to rub on my "pearl". My mom taught me that no one was supposed to touch down there and if they did, it was my job to tell an adult. I wondered if he knew what he was doing. I wondered if he knew he wasn't supposed to touch my "pearl". I said, "No daddy, don't touch that". He slapped my hand down, grabbed me out of my bed and brought me into the bedroom he shared with my mom. I began to cry, and he said, "Do you want me to beat you? You better not wake your sister up". I'm still so confused at this very moment because I didn't understand. What did I do? Why was he doing this to me? He threw me in the bed and said don't move. He said if you make a sound, I'll kill your sister and your mother. I tried to hold my tears in the best way I could. He grabbed a tape to put into the VCR. Once it came on, there were people doing nasty things to each other. I put my hands over my eyes because my grandmother would always make us turn our heads or put our hands over our eyes for the nasty parts of movies. He slapped my hands and told me I needed to watch it so that I could learn what to do. He laid on side of me and touched all over my body. He tried to put his finger inside of my "pearl". It hurt so bad. I asked him to stop. I cried for him to stop. He wouldn't stop. That perfect man who had come into our lives; who I thought was superman, in that very moment, became something scarier than the boogeyman that was in my closet and under my bed. My life was completely changed that night. He said he was doing this to me because he loved me, and it had to be our little secret because a lot of people could get hurt. He made me touch his private area. He told me to pet it like a dog. I started to get nauseated as the porno played loudly in the background. He grabbed my hand and wrapped it around himself and began going up and down as he watched the video. After he finished, he ran me some bath water and put me in the tub. He washed me off and told me that he loved me and to remember that it was our secret. I wanted to scream, but I was overwhelmed with fear. He dried me off, put a fresh pair of night clothes on me and tucked me in bed. I didn't even close my eyes to go to sleep because I kept replaying what happened over and over in my head. I couldn't wait until my mom got home so that I could tell her what happened. I quickly remembered that he said he would hurt them if I did. I didn't know what to do. My private area was hurting. I grabbed my teddy bear and hugged it tight and fell asleep.

The next morning, I heard my mom come in. I jumped out of the bed and ran into the front room, only to find him dressed for work and standing next to my mom. He was hugging and kissing her and telling her to have a good day, but when he saw me standing there, he paused for a moment and waited to see what I was going to do. I hesitated for a moment before I approached my mom. I walked slowly towards her and hugged her tightly. She said, "Somebody must miss me". She had no idea how much. She just didn't know how true that statement was. I wanted to cry out to her and tell her, but he gave me this look that I'll never forget. That look silenced me. He walked out of the door and left for work. My mother was just getting in from work so of course, she went rest for a while before cooking and cleaning. As she rested, I tried to come up with a plan on how to tell her that he touched my "pearl". His voice kept speaking loudly to me in my ear; saying, "If you say anything, I will kill your mother and sister". Then, I would be like the little orphan Annie. Maybe some rich family would adopt me. My thoughts ran wild that entire morning. My baby sister finally woke up. My mom asked me to take her in the backyard to play while she rested a little. Here I am, sitting under this big magnolia tree. I was crumbling the leaves in my hands and watching the wind take it away. My little sister was sitting in the grass playing with her doll. I went sit next to her and asked her if someone ever touched her "pearl". She shook her head no. I took a deep breath and told her what happened to me. She didn't quite understand what I was saying. Her response warranted a hug from me. She said, "It's ok, Nunny. You can sleep with me tonight, so the big bad monster won't steal you out of the bed". I wasn't certain if it would happen again, but I accepted her offer with joy.

My New Orleans family was still at my grandmother's house visiting, but I never got a chance to see them for the rest of the break. I guess my stepdad was afraid I would say something because we spent the rest of the Thanksgiving break with him. On a normal day, he would be so anxious to drop us off. He didn't come into my room again for the rest of that week and I thought things were back to normal. Before I knew it, the Thanksgiving break was coming to an end. That Sunday night, my mom ironed my school clothes.

I was excited to see my friends at school on Monday and to hear all of their interesting stories from their break. I got in the bed with my sister thinking I was safe. I actually laid down behind her. I knew for sure that I would have a good night just like the other nights, but I was wrong. You ever fall into a deep sleep, but something wakes you up and startles you? Well imagine that happening and you're no longer in the room you fell asleep in. Yes, he took me out of bed and brought me into their bedroom again. This time, I screamed at the top of my lungs, and I begged him to let me go back to our room. He grabbed a sock and some duct tape. He stuffed the sock in my mouth and put the duct tape over my mouth to hold the sock in. He put that same movie on with the people having sex. He grabbed the back of my head and made me watch it. As the tears ran down my face, I started to daydream. I didn't want to watch this. I didn't understand why he was doing this again. How could Superman be such a villain? I daydreamed that I was in Paris. I was walking the runway with my poodle. My name was Chi-Chi Rodriguez. My grandmother was a movie fanatic. We watched "To Wong Foo, Thanks for Everything! Julie Newmar" a few weeks prior and I fell in love with Chi-Chi. Right when I was getting to the end of the runway, dressed in my orange leather mini skirt, I felt a lot of pain in my private area. He was trying to penetrate me. He said, "Keep still". How could I? I cried as his sweat dripped on my face. I could barely breathe with the sock in my mouth and him laying on top of me. He was a big man.

He had two big chemical burns on the side of his face. I think he got hurt on a job or something. It looked so nasty. He began to look like a monster, as he rubbed my face while moving his body up and down; saying, "I love you and this is our little secret". He couldn't get inside of me, it seemed like the more he tried, the more he would get upset with me. After trying for what seemed like forever, he finally stopped. He took the tape from over my mouth and took the sock out. I took a deep breath and he brought me into the bathroom. He ran my bath water and told me to sit in the water and soak. He said he would be back in a little while to bathe me. I sat in the water, but something made me get out of the tub and look in the mirror. I wanted to see myself. My face was so red, and my eyes were very puffy. No one had ever taught me anything about suicide. I didn't even know what it was to want to kill yourself. All I knew was that I wanted to die. Living just seemed unfair. I thought, maybe because I didn't have a real daddy, this is what happens to little girls who don't have real daddies. He walked back in the bathroom and said, "Stop playing around. Get back in the tub". He soaped the towel and began scrubbing me down. He patted between my legs with the towel. I guess he saw the way my face grimaced, as I opened my legs. He had that same talk with me that he had with me the last time. You know that talk about how it was a secret. That he loved me. So, on and so on. I was over it. This was my punishment for not having a father. I deserved this. Real daddies don't touch their daughter's "pearls". He dried me off. He dressed me and tucked me into bed. He kissed me on my cheek and told me he loved me.

That morning, my mom woke me up for school and I was hoping that she would notice something different about me. I thought mommies had superpowers. I mean she always knew when I was lying and when I was telling the truth. She knew if I was happy or sad. I thought she would instantly know what was going on with me. She dressed me for school, and she didn't say anything. She didn't say a thing! She didn't even ask me how I was feeling. Maybe she thought I was just tired, or her superpowers were broken. Maybe, my stepdad turned her superpowers off. I'm just ready to get to school. She hugged me and sent me out the door. The elementary school I went to was right next to the projects, but when my mom got married, we moved across town from it. So, I became a car rider. That left "you know who" in charge of bringing me to school. He had a white 2 door Oldsmobile. My mom handed me my book sack and said, "Have a great day beautiful girl". I didn't feel like that beautiful girl anymore, but she just didn't see it. I walked to the car, holding the straps of my book sack really tight. I just knew that ride to school would be so awkward. When I got in the car, my mom was standing in the door waving at me. My stepdad reached over to buckle my seat belt. Instantly, I got fearful and I thought my mom would see my face, but she just closed the door. He adjusted my seatbelt slowly and it disturbed my little soul. That ride was creepy and lengthy. Maybe my anxiety was making the ride seem longer. When we pulled up to the car rider line, he had that pep talk with me again about keeping our secret. He said if I told my teacher that he could get in big trouble and really bad things would happen to my mom and sister. I shook my head "yes" and I grabbed the door handle to get out of the car. He grabbed my arm and gave me an evil look just to let me know that he wasn't playing with me. I got out of the car and as I walked down the walkway, I watched his car pull away. I wanted to run to my grandmother's house and fall into her arms. Even if I didn't have a real daddy, I knew she would protect me. My grandfather was bigger than my stepdad. If I told my grandfather, he would peel his head. As I'm walking and thinking, I hear my friends saying my name.

I had and still have the best friends in the whole wide world. Cliff is my best friend. He had a really big head and big teeth, but I always thought his head was so big because he's so smart. Then, there's Mya. She was so tiny and cute like a little mouse. Kate had the prettiest hair. She looked like Susie from "Rugrats", and she was very loud. When she laughed, you definitely heard it. Nadia was my play sister. We called each other real sisters, but everyone knew we were lying because her mom was white, and my mom was black. Kerri and I had this love hate relationship. We were friends, but I would tease her from time to time. It wasn't personal. I just had to take the heat off myself. I was just doing to her what other people did to me. I loved her, but I could've left the fat jokes out of it. Hurt people hurt people no matter the age. Bianca was my girl too. She was super smart and stayed to herself. She was always so kind to everyone. That was my crew. We thought we were colder than cold cups. Cliff's mom and my grandmother would let us talk on the phone sometimes. He was more like a brother to me.

Chapter 2

In the mornings, we would sit in the hallway and wait for the morning bell to ring. It was like a little morning recess break. Me and my crew sat in front of the office. That particular morning, everybody had big smiles on their faces, as I approached them. Cliff smelled really good that day. He admitted that he used his mom's Vagisil feminine spray. I could've sworn I saw my mom spray that on her private area, but he put some on his neck and wrist as if it was perfume or cologne. I told him a few days later that it was coochie spray. We laughed about it. We were always laughing with each other. He thought it was perfume. That moment took my mind completely away from the horrors I was facing at home. I wanted to tell my friends about my thanksgiving break, but I didn't want to ruin our reunion. The bell finally rang, and it was time to go to class.

My first-grade teacher's name was Mrs. Walters. She was like 6 feet tall. Not really, but she wore stilettos every day. She blasted gospel music and put holy oil on our foreheads as soon as we walked through the door. She didn't just talk. She yelled. It was like we were in a holy boot camp. I was very talkative. It wasn't my fault. I just couldn't help it. She would say, "Wells" which is my last name, by the way. "Wells, go grab that ruler". She never sent us to the principal's office. She popped our little butts with that ruler so hard, and I tell you no lie, she never broke a nail. Not once! She taught my mom when she was in elementary school, also. Being that my mom was 14 years old when she had me, Mrs. Walters understood what generational curses were. Now that I'm older, I appreciate her for constantly telling me that I wasn't going to be like my mother. At first, I took it as an insult. I thought she was trying to embarrass me or look down on me, but that wasn't the case. She knew the importance of speaking things into existence. The Bible says that life and death is in the power of our tongues. She was breaking curses off of my life and I didn't even know it. She would even make me miss recess if I didn't do what I was supposed to do.

Recess was my favorite part of school. Just to run around and play on the playground was my favorite thing to do. There was a water fountain that didn't work well. We called it the, "buger water fountain", and if anyone touched it or drank from it, everyone would say they had the "coodies". A little boy on the playground decided to lie and say I drank from it. I was on the slide. I don't know why he decided to come for me. Whelp, now for the next week, I'd be known as the "buger water" girl.

After school each day, I walked to my grandmother's house, but before getting to her house, I would stop by my grandmother's best friend, Ms. Dee. She owned the neighborhood corner store. Her house was connected to the store. Her son and I were thick as thieves. She sold boudin, hot dogs, chips and groceries. Every day after school, I would get my free chips and juice. And sometimes, she gave me a ham and cheese po'boy. Those were the best. It felt like the cheese was made in cheese heaven. After that, I made my way to my grandmother and grandfather's apartment.

My grandfather worked offshore. He would be gone for months at a time, but when he was home, it was nothing in the world he wouldn't buy for us. I was hoping he was home, but he wasn't. My Uncle David was home. He's my mother's little brother. My Uncle David was so cool. He watched cartoons with me. He would make me watch Dragon Ball Z with him. I hated that cartoon. I wanted to watch The Little Mermaid, but I enjoyed his company anyway. He would make us egg sandwiches, and we would sit on the floor in front of the TV. I thought about telling him what happened to me over the Thanksgiving break, but I was just so scared of what would happen. Fear can really stop us from being free. F.E.A.R stands for "False Evidence Appearing Real". He made me think in my mind that if I said something, I would get in trouble and I believed him. How could I be so stupid? How did I let him get into my thoughts? And here I go blaming myself. I blamed myself for it all. It was all my fault.

I watched the clock the whole time while at my grandmother's house. I was waiting very anxiously for my stepdad to get off and pick me up. I dreaded it. When he finally pulled up, I heard his horn blowing. If what I was feeling showed on my face, my uncle noticed. He asked me if everything was ok. I told him I was ok, but I could tell he didn't believe me. He said if anyone is hurting you, please don't be afraid to let me know. I said ok, but I still didn't tell him anything. I just grabbed my book sack and walked out slowly. When I got to the car, he asked me what took so long. I lied and said that I couldn't find my book sack. He said, "Who did you talk to today?". I said, "No one". He said, "You're lying. I know you did, and I'll have to punish you when we get home". I swore to God that I didn't tell anyone. I really didn't. He was making it up just to do what he wanted to do to me. I know that now, but he was very convincing; always making me second guess myself. When we got home, I took my time getting out of the car. He grabbed me by my jacket and rushed me out of the car. When we got in the house, he slammed the door and said take off all your clothes. I started crying and said no. "Please don't make me do it! Please, I'm sorry! I didn't say anything! I swear!" He slapped me. That was the first time he had ever hit me. That was the first time I'd ever got slapped in the face. I wasn't a bad child, so my family never really had to fuss at me or even come close to whipping me. My face turned hot and I cried harder. He said, "If you don't stop that crying, I'm going to give you something to cry about". I tried to suck it up the best way I could. I started taking my clothes off, but I guess I was taking too long. He grabbed me and pulled my pants down. He laid me on the floor and started kissing me on my private area. I cried and cried and cried. I cried for my momma. He slapped my face again and told me to stop crying before the neighbors hear me. I put my hand over my mouth to try to keep quiet, but I just couldn't stop crying. He told me to sit up. He told me to put my mouth on his private area. I didn't know what to do or what he was asking me to do. He told me to kiss it. He grabbed me by my neck, choked me and told me to kiss it. I didn't do it. I didn't want to do it. He slapped me again. This time my nose started to bleed. He dragged me to the bathroom and sat me down in the tub. He ran my bath water. As the water was running, he went in his room and I heard the nasty movie playing loudly. I felt my eyes swelling from crying so much. I had a headache. I couldn't get my nose to stop bleeding. I leaned over to turn the water off, and I grabbed a towel and held it on my nose. I guess once he finished touching himself, he came back in the bathroom and bathed me. He said, "If your momma asks what happened to you, you need to say that you fell playing in the backyard". I shook my head "yes". He said, "Are you going to tell on me?" I shook my head "yes". He proceeded to tell me that my mom wouldn't believe me. He laughed at me. He really looked at me and laughed. Once he dried me off and put my clothes on, he left out of the bathroom. I looked in the mirror and saw that my bottom lip was swollen. My right cheek had scratches on it. My little eyes were puffy, and my cheeks were red like roses. I was ugly…inside and out. I felt it. My grandmother always told me how beautiful I was. She drowned me in compliments. All of that immediately went away as I looked in the mirror. He handed me my bed clothes.

After he would sexually, mentally and physically abuse me, he would act as if nothing happened. My mom really believed that I fell and fussed at me for being clumsy. She almost whipped me. It's something about black mothers I never understood. They will whip you for having an accident. I mean children are supposed to fall, scrape their knees and trip over things. I was so mad! How could she not know what was happening to me? How could she be so blind? When have I ever hurt myself? I'm always careful. She believed anything he said. If he said the sky was purple, she would believe that too. Now he knew he had me. Instead of it being sometimes, it became an everyday thing. As soon as I got from school, he had a routine. He forced me to take off my clothes. He kissed me, touched me and made me watch nasty movies. He would make me touch and kiss him, also. Years and years passed by and it never stopped. He was always trying to get inside of my "pearl", but he couldn't. It would make him angry. He would bathe me and put me to bed. He would kiss me on my forehead and tell me that he loved me. After a while, it started to become normal until I turned 8 years old. I'm turning the combination on my padlock again.

While at school one day, Mother Nature decided to bless me with a gift. A gift that caused me to be teased. I mean, I was only in the 3rd grade. On this particular day, right after we ate lunch, my teacher told me that I had something on the back of my pants. She didn't tell me discreetly. She said it so loud that the whole class heard her. Everyone laughed. So, now I'm being called Bloody Mary. Life was great! I'm totally being sarcastic. My grandmother came to check me out of school, and she had the talk with me about menstruation. She said every woman gets them. I asked why? And, I asked if I was going to die. I mean, that much blood coming from down there, and I'm supposed to wear these miniature pampers inside of my panties? Who thought of this and why do we have to have periods? Periods are supposed to end a sentence, not come out of your body. She made me some soup because my stomach was cramping and gave me some liquid Tylenol. I've been hungry before, but this was worse than hunger pains. I rested the entire day. I had to walk and meet my little sister at the gate later that day. She was in school now. As soon as I got to the gate, the other kids said we heard you got your period. Dang, word travels fast. Jesus Christ! How did everyone know that fast? They laughed and called me Bloody Mary, but I didn't care. I always tried my best not to care about what anyone says about me. Sometimes it's hard to pretend. My grandmother taught me that sticks and stones may break my bones, but words would never hurt me. That wasn't true because words did hurt.

We did our daily routine. We walked to the corner store, got our afternoon snack and went home. When we got back home, my aunt teased me about it too. She said, "Uggghhh you nasty". So now I'm bleeding and it's nasty. I just wish the world would end already. I know she was only joking, but I had so much going on already. I just wanted to get home. I needed to sit under my tree and watch the wind blow the leaves away.

My stepdad pulled up and started blowing his horn outside. As we rode home, I was thinking to myself. Should I tell him that I got my period? I was just unsure if I should or not. I didn't really talk to him since he'd started molesting me. I didn't sit on his lap anymore. I didn't tell him good morning or ask him to help me ride my bike. I tried my best to stay out of his way as much as I could. When we got home, he asked me if I was feeling bad because I didn't look well. I shook my head "yes". He told me I could go lay down and that we would have our play date tomorrow. He had the nerve to call what he was doing a "play date"! A play date! I was just happy that I got to go lay down without any problems. My stomach was hurting so bad anyways. Having a "play date" with him would've made it worse. I could barely sleep that night because I was scared that he would come get me out of my bed. Thank God he didn't. I heard him watching his nasty movies though. It seemed like as soon as I closed my eyes, it was daytime again. My mom woke me up to make sure I was ok. She said that I could stay home from school that day because of my menstrual cycle. She wanted to teach me about changing my pads and how to take care of myself properly. I was excited to spend the day with her. My stepdad left to bring my baby sister to school. I thought he would've been off to work after that, but he came right back home. I overheard him tell my mom that he called out of work to stay home and spend some time with her. He only did that so he could monitor the things I said in front of her. I got dressed and went sit outside under my favorite magnolia tree. I crumbled the leaves in my hands and watched the wind take them away.

I pretended that I was on the magic school bus. Reading books was a hobby of mine. Ramona Quimby was all of that and a bag of chips. My godmother would always take me to the bookstore to get books. She's my mom's best friend. My nanny was in college to be a nurse, but she always made sure I had gifts and books. That day, I was sitting under the tree reading a book, and I saw my stepdad walk outside. He had an evil look on his face. He walked up to me, angrily. He slapped my book out of my hand, picked me up in the air and shook me. He said, "Why didn't you tell me you have a period?". I said I don't know why. He shakes me and squeezes my arms real hard. He yelled, "You can get pregnant". He throws me down to the ground. Of course, I started to cry. My mom came outside to see why I was crying. He told her he spanked me because I was hurting the dog. She believed him and fussed at me again. I got up, dusted myself off and kicked the leaves. My silence was consuming me. I was screaming on the inside and no one could hear me. When my little sister got home from school, I told her what happened to me. I mean, she's only

5 years old, but I just needed to let it out. Her response was, "It's ok. You can sleep with me. That way I can feel if he's coming get you out of the bed, and I can scream really loud for him to stop". She hugged me and we cried together. Surely, that's what happened. I slept with her and she hugged me tight like a teddy bear. He didn't come in the room that night because I was still going through my cycle. After about 4 days of bleeding, I knew what time it was. I knew he was coming for me. I could tell by the way he looked at me. He asked if I was still bleeding in front of my mom and sister and made it seem as if he was joking. I knew the real reason was so that we could have his "play date".

My behavior started to change. I wasn't just the talkative comedian anymore. I started to act out and misbehave in school. I'm sure you're wondering why I turned my padlock at this age if the same abuse continued. Something different happens here. I got in trouble at school. They called my mom to let her know I was going to be sent to detention. I was disrespecting the teachers and so were my peers. Cliff always had my back no matter what. This time, we both were in trouble. I've always loved to read and write. I took an extra tablet I had and created a story about sex, lies and relationships. The characters were my friends. They would pass the tablet around and everyone would read it, as I wrote each chapter. Cliff decided to draw the pictures to go with the book. He drew people having sex and kissing. A teacher became suspicious about us passing around a book, and she confiscated it. She brought it to the principal's office. All I could think was, "That's your ass, Mr. Postman". I just knew I was in trouble when I got home. There was one thing my family didn't play about and that was school. You had to get your education. So many people before my generation didn't have a diploma. They made it extra hard on us to break that cycle. When I got home, my mom talked to me about my behavior. Black mommas whip you and then ask you why, while you're crying. How can I answer after you just knocked me out? I never understood that, but after she whipped me like I stole something, I opened my mouth and told her everything. I told her that he had been touching me. I told her how he had touched me. I told her what he does to me when she's not there. I told her how much it hurt. She started crying, and I felt this big weight being lifted off my shoulders. She sat there in silence. She didn't say a word. It was like she was waiting for something. We sat there together crying and waiting. After a while, I realized that she was waiting for him. Even though I'd told on him, hearing his car pull up put fear in my heart because I didn't know what was going to happen. I thought she would've asked me to go to my room so that they could talk, but she didn't. As soon as he walked in the room, she said, "You been touching on my child". He looked at me and looked back at my mom and swore to her that I was lying. He told her that I must be mad with him about something. She paused for a moment. I kept saying, "Momma, I'm not lying". She stood up and looked me dead in my eyes and told me that I was making this up because I wanted her to be with my biological father. The weight that I thought fell off my shoulders came back 10 times heavier. How could she think that? How could she not believe me? I didn't even know who my daddy was. I'd never spent time with him or his family. I just knew his name. How could that possibly be a reason? She sent me to my room. I heard him fussing at her. I couldn't make out what he was saying though. All I could think is that he'd won. There is no escaping this. This is complete torture. There I was AGAIN, crumbling the leaves in my hands and watching the wind take it away.

The next morning my mom woke me up and asked if I wanted to go live with my grandmother. Of course, I said, "Yes". We started packing my clothes. I didn't see my stepdad in the house. He must've left for work. She brought me to my grandmother's. The ride there was very quiet. When I got to my grandmother's house, she had a room set up for me. My uncle had moved out and moved in with his girlfriend. My aunt was there visiting. She would be back and forth. My aunt was so fine; like Diamond from "The Players Club" fine. She had a short haircut like Eve the rapper. She had the paw prints tattooed on her breast, as well. I guess that was the thing back then. My mom dropped me off and left. My aunt asked if my stepdad had been touching me. I said yes. She smirked and said okay. I guess she didn't believe me either. She walked away and started rolling up some weed with her friends. I walked through the hallway and went put my things away, in the room. I took a deep breath. I was free. I was finally away from him. Well, at least I thought I was. Even when people aren't physically present, they could possibly still be with you. If we are too young to understand forgiveness, our hurt can transform us into becoming our worst enemy. You start doing things that don't benefit your wellbeing.

For bath time, I would run my water and just sit on the toilet. I didn't want to get in the bathtub anymore. I didn't understand why back then, but now I understand it was because of the trauma. Every time he touched me; he'd bathe me right after he finished. I felt dirty on the inside, so I wanted to feel dirty on the outside. Unaware of my entire feelings, I just didn't want to take a bath. The children at school would say I was stink. They called me musty. When the school called my grandmother to let her know that I was being teased, she didn't understand because she thought I was bathing when I'd go in the bathroom. She just wrote it off as the kids being mean. I never cried when I was bullied. I developed thick skin, and it just made me act out even more. I had to force myself not to care, to numb myself. I told myself that if I didn't have feelings, then nothing could hurt me. I was a walking bullet proof vest. I could still feel the sting from the shots though.

Chapter 3

Ms. Judy was the disciplinarian of our school, and my friend Kate's great aunt. I was always with her because I stayed in troubled. My mouth was doing so much. I said things I shouldn't have said. At one point, I had my friends in the bathroom touching an invisible baby. Kate was the only person who took me seriously. I'm laughing now thinking about it. She really was giving me baby names in the 3rd grade and rubbing my stomach as if there was a baby growing inside of me. She said, "Ya'll I can feel the baby kicking". We were a mess. Ms. Judy monitored us for lunch, and she would scream in the lunchroom, "I smell a gorilla". That meant she heard someone talking. We were supposed to be quiet the whole time we were in the lunchroom. Of course, I would lose my lunch recess because I had to be the gorilla that was talking. She would ask, "Do you want Fletcher or Bolden? Choose one". That's the names of funeral homes, Ya'll. And, you'd better not get caught asking anybody for their chocolate milk. You were going sit at her table and you got a free pass to detention with her. She had the longest fingernails, and they were her real nails. She always had the latest fashion. I would look at her and say to myself when I grow up, I'm making sure I dress like that. I landed myself in detention that week because I started a rumor that my teacher and the principal were having an affair. I also came to school with a thong on and told everyone on the playground that I had one on. What was I thinking? I was suffering from abandonment issues. I hadn't seen my mom since she dropped me off. I wanted attention and was going about it the wrong way. While in detention, Ms. Judy let me know how she felt about me hanging with her niece, my good friend Kate. She told me not to play with her or sit with her. That made me feel really bad on top of how I was already feeling. Ms. Judy didn't understand or know what I was dealing with at home. She told me she was going to rearrange my classes. Because of our last names, Kate and I were always in class together. She made it happen. Kate still would talk to me and remained my friend. Ms. Judy thought I was acting like a misbehaved project kid. She thought I was just being a product of my environment. I was being raised by a college educated woman and a kind and generous man, my grandmother and grandfather, but I was violated and that angered me. I didn't love myself anymore. So why should I care about my future.

Luke 8:43-48 tells us a story about the woman with the issue of blood. She had a bleeding condition for 12 years. And for the life of me, I couldn't understand why she had to be isolated. It was a law in those times that commanded her not to be in contact with people because if they touched her, they would have the issue too. Matthew 5:13 says, "You are the salt of the earth: but if the salt loses its saltiness, how can it be made salty again? It is no longer good for anything, except to be thrown out and trampled underfoot." What I've learned about salt is that it stops meat from bleeding. When God calls us salt, He's calling us "preservers". If I'm not salty, then I'm bleeding. Blood leaks and flows. I was able to forgive those people who didn't want me around because now I understand that principle. I had issues, and I was leaking out on others. I was contaminating their purity. Even though I was crying out for help, it still was not my place to bleed out on others. That's a personal journey. It's ok to heal, but you can't cause others to hurt in the process. The woman with the issue of blood tried everything that she could to fix her issue, and so was I. Nothing worked. She spent a lot of money with doctors trying to repair herself. It was not until she heard about a man named Jesus that she pressed her way through the crowd just to touch the hem of his garment. The Bible says, immediately she was healed. I was still so young. I had no idea that pressing my way through the crowd would be so hard. I had no way of knowing that I needed to get my salt back. So, I continued to bleed and bleed. I continued to find all the wrong ways. I was condemned for it. Criticized and beaten down because of it. My only peace of mind was going to my nanny's house on weekends.

She had an apartment in Lafayette, and there was a pool. My cousin Anna and I, which is my nanny's baby sister, would go every weekend. She was 3 years older than me. I considered her a big sister. I called her Penny from "Good Times". She looked like Janet Jackson when she was a little girl. Her hair was curly and pretty. I don't think her skin color is a real color. You know those people that you can't say they're light skinned or dark skinned? They're not caramel. It's like that weird in between color, but it's pretty. She was beautiful. She lived in the projects too, but you could never tell. She always had the latest Jordan's and best clothes. Her mom, my Aunt Stella, was my grandmother's best friend. My Aunt Stella lived in our backyard, the apartment right behind ours. I spent a lot of time there. Anna always had cool stuff. Even though I would pee on everything, she would say, "You can't come sleep over here anymore". Somehow, I found myself back over there all the time. My mom said when I was a baby, she came over to see me and my momma told her that she couldn't because I was sleeping. Anna said, "Nobody wants to see yo' ugly, bald-headed baby anyway" and slammed the door. My momma said she woke me up because in the projects we had big iron screen doors. Even though she called me ugly, we were always thick as thieves. We even got beat up together. One girl beat both of us up at the same time, and we'd just put a fresh perm. Our hair was full of dirt. It was Anna's idea to call Deanna fat and I teamed in, of course. Yup, that's right she beat us both at the same time. My momma jokingly asked if we even pinched her. She always had a joke. We were dusty from head to toe. That's my girl though. I wouldn't have wanted to get beat up with anyone else.

Besides the issues at school and not seeing my mom as often as I'd liked, my grandmother tried her best to spoil me. I got anything I wanted. My godmother would try her best too. I looked forward to her sending me books and picking me up on weekends. I just wanted to feel different on the inside. I finally got some relief from my depression. My mom came back for me. She was leaving my stepdad. Not because he molested me though. Speaking of which, no one seemed to talk to me about that situation one bit, not even my grandmother. She decided to leave him because he was cheating on her. She got an apartment in Iberia Village Apartment complex. Driving into it was rough being that there were rocks and potholes everywhere. I was excited. It's nothing like having your mother around. I wanted to be with my little sister again. My mom seemed liberated. She was in her own place and was doing it on her own. My little sister and I had our room together and my mom had her own room in a cozy 2-bedroom apartment. Everything was amazing. My mom was a hardcore Christian. We went to a church called Joy Tabernacle. That's where I met my good friend Mitchell. His grandmother was the pastor of the church, Pastor Nelson. Her oldest daughter was one of my mom's best friends. Her name was Helen. She lived in the same apartment complex as we did with her 2 daughters and her son. I would pretend to catch the Holy Ghost, so that I could get peppermints and attention. I know it was so wrong, but hey, I'm a kid and I have issues. Pastor Nelson didn't play at all. This was a time when women preaching wasn't popular or even accepted. She broke so many barriers. I saw these women cry and lay at the alter all day and night. She wouldn't leave the church until you were healed and delivered. She baptized people. She would straight lay you out at the altar. I loved it there, but it seemed like my mom stopped going to church when we moved in those apartments. Her and her good friend Helen, the pastor's oldest daughter, would go out to the clubs. They had another friend who lived in the same apartments named Naomi. She had about 4 children that we played with. Ms. Naomi cooked really good. My favorite was corn and rice with smothered pork chops. I don't know who taught her how to cook, but she was the best at it. Sometimes, our momma would leave us at her house for days. She would comb our hair and let us watch cartoons. Helen's oldest daughter, Amina, watched us sometimes too. Even though my mom was living her best life, I can't say that we didn't have a blast. We would pretend that we were in the club and blasted the music in the apartment. We used sodas and pretended it was beer. Amina would comb everybody's hair and dress us up, and she would feed us too. She had to be at least 12 years old at the time. Those types of children always turn out to be great mothers. I think it's because their nurturing side kicks in early. That's an amazing thing. She would have fun with us and fuss at us within the same hour.

I don't know why my momma put Allison, my little sister, a curl. That curl would drip everywhere. I came up with this song called "follow the drip", and I would sing it all the time. My baby sister had gotten so much bigger than me. She was taller and chunkier, so I had to pick on her because I was scared that one day, she would knock me out. We were at Helen's house for the night. They were all going out again. My friend Mitchell is Helen's son. Amina is his oldest sister. We all decided to take a sheet and wrap it around me as a wedding dress. She did my hair and make up for my big day. My groom was Mitchell. He was standing there smiling hard with that big head. She wrapped that sheet around me tightly. The wedding song that I walked down the hallway to was "Meeting in my Bedroom" by Silk. Ok, I know it's not the ideal wedding song, but it was the only CD Ms. Helen had. We had to work with what we had. As I approached my "husband" with my plastic flower in my hand, I was preparing to say "I do" just so I could kiss him. As soon as I got close to him and Amina read our vows, I kissed him before she could even finish. Next, it was time for our honeymoon in the closet. We were supposed to be humping in the closet, Ya'll. We just sat there. We sat there and looked at each other. I'm glad we didn't do anything because sitting in that closet reminded me of the times I hid in the closet from my stepdad. I tried to bury those memories. Something always comes back to remind you of unfortunate events of the past. Everybody thought we did something in the closet, and we just let them think that.

We were watching the time because Ms. Helen always made sure her house was clean. We had to make sure everything was clean before they got back from the club. We scattered like roaches when the lights were cut on, running here and there to make sure the house was clean. Finally, we finished and sat on the sofa and pretended to be watching TV the entire time. They really believed that we were little angels. Amina would put my hair in the prettiest donut. A donut is a hair style in which you take a sock, cut it and roll it into a donut shape. You put your hair in a ponytail and lay your hair over the sock. I didn't even think my hair could do that, but she always made me look nice. She made me feel pretty again. I lost that feeling along the way. I don't think she knew that just by simply giving me a few shirts to put on and combing my hair was helping break down a lot of my insecurities. Besides blaming myself for my abuse, I lost my confidence.

My mom met this new guy. He was from out of town. My sister and I really liked him. He would give her money to buy us things and she would take us places. We went to K-mart and put so much stuff in the basket. Only to find out that she was putting it on lay-away. Man, that was so aggravating. Mothers should go to the store by themselves when they plan on doing that. I mean, you're asking me to pick stuff out that I can't take home at that very moment.

That's stupid, but if I got to spend time with her, I didn't mind. We would go eat pizza. She'd take us to the park and riding with her to different cities. My mom and her friends drank wine coolers and took us riding around town. I used to have my flavored water, pretending that it was a wine cooler. I also pretended like I was drunk. My drunk impersonations were everything. I pretended not to know who I was or where I was and walked as if I was about to fall. We had so much fun until one day my mom was in bed with her new friend. I was laying on the sofa watching TV. I heard something by our door, but I didn't pay it any mind. About 5 minutes later, our front door opened, and it was my stepdad. He put his hand over his lips signaling for me to be quiet. I wanted to scream my momma's name, but I was stuck. He hid in the closet in our room. I sat there and pee'd on myself. He had a baseball bat in his hand when he walked in. I remembered when he told me that if I told anyone about our "play dates", he would kill me, my mom and my sister. My mom's new boyfriend got out of the bed to go to the bathroom, and my stepdad ran out of our room and started beating the man with the bat. My mom screamed stop, and she was crying. I got up and ran in the room by her. She was clutching the blanket on her naked body and screaming for help as my stepdad bashed her boyfriend's head in. Allison cried and cried. She was hiding in the closet. When she came out of the closet, my stepdad and my mother's boyfriend ran into her, as they scuffled. She was knocked into the wall. She hit her head on the wall, but they kept fighting. Thankfully, the neighbors called the cops and my stepdad ran out of the house. My stepdad had to be watching them and strategizing the right moment to come in. I don't know what my mom told the cops. I never saw her boyfriend again. I really liked him. We hadn't seen our grandparents in a while because my grandfather worked offshore, and my grandmother never learned how to drive. She literally walked everywhere she went. That day, we went spend time with my grandmother so we could get away from our apartment for the day. We needed a break. My stepdad knocked down everything during the fight. Our cozy little apartment was turned inside out.

It felt good being in the projects by my grandma. I got to play with all my friends in her neighborhood. Phaedra and Kirsten were my best friends. I had other friends, but they were my girls. Before me and Kirsten became friends, she slapped me after school one day because I snitched on her for cutting the lunch line. I was so scared to walk home from school that day because she told me she was going to slap me after school. I tried to get home quickly, but she stopped me right in my tracks. I walked home feeling so embarrassed. Everybody was laughing. They were like "Aww man, you not gon' do nothing". I just stood there playing with the straps on my backpack. Kirsten looked at me like, "What you wanna do?". I didn't run, but I walked home really fast. Later that year, we became sisters. We shared some of the same struggles with our mothers. She became my confidant and if you messed with me, she was coming for you. It's crazy how I feared her when we first met; not realizing that we needed each other. That was a big lesson learned. I now know that the enemy despises divine connections. I finally had someone in my corner that understood my struggle. We were enemies turned into sisters. She took me under her wing.

Winter

This is the darkest and coldest time of year. It's so quiet, you can hear a pin drop. If you stay still enough, you just might get stuck in the cold and darkness. Hearts may get colder and harder. Hibernation may be necessary. Walking in the cold and darkness can be hard because you're going up against the wind.

Chapter 4

We started packing up to move out of our apartment in Iberia Village. I was going to miss my friends back there. My mom never let me get in the pool there, but I was going to miss watching everybody swim. We packed up everything, got a storage unit to put everything in, and we left. We could've stayed with my grandmother, but I guess that wasn't a part of my mother's plan. We moved in with one of her friends named Kendra. Kendra had long legs, and she loved her short shorts. She was tall and slender, but she had a nice shape. She had a daughter named Megan. Megan was her only child, and she was super spoiled. She had eczema on her knees and elbows. That was the first time I ever saw anything like that. In my mind, I thought she may have fallen and scraped her skin. She had a pretty smile and long puffy hair. She had so many toys in her room that we were not allowed to touch. Her mom was funny about stuff like that. My mom, myself and my sister shared a room. Ms. Kendra had a 3-bedroom apartment in the projects. The apartment complex was called Bacmonalia. She would always tell me how fine I was. I didn't believe her because it seemed like someone was calling me ugly, gravel face or pepperoni face every other day. My facial acne was doing the most. They even called me connect the dot face. So, I'm turning the combination on my padlock again. Living with Ms. Kendra was cool, but we couldn't eat Megan's snacks or play with her toys. She would have Rice Krispy Treats, my favorite snack, Ya'll. We couldn't have any. My momma had a new boyfriend. He would walk us to the Asian market to get our own snacks. His name was Mr. Ernie. He would buy us ice cream from Viator's Drive-In too. Viator's had the best burgers, hot dogs and po'boys. It was on Hopkin Street, not too far from Bacmonalia. He would even comb our hair. We walked to Viator's every Friday. I enjoyed those days. Our new stepdad was madly in love with my mom. I knew because he looked at her and his eyes glistened. I could tell my mom didn't feel the same way. I don't think she felt good enough for him. My mom had it going on. She was dark-skinned with beautiful teeth and that stank walk I inherited. Not only did I have bad acne, I walked like a duck. Well at least that's what the children at school would say about me. I lied and said I had scoliosis. I really believed I did. Nobody ever took me to get it checked out though. Since I was the oldest, I had to babysit Allison and Megan. My momma and Kendra went out a lot. I was in charge. I tried to remember all the things Amina did when she watched us, but this time they would leave for days at a time. We would run out of food, so I invented a combination of rice, butter and sugar. That was the best thing in the world, especially if you're hungry. I would give everybody a rice krispy treat as dessert.

Sometimes, Megan left to go by her family members. When my mom was home, I would leave her and my little sister in the apartment. I liked to roam around the complex. There was a dance team in the complex. I would sit in the grass and watch them practice. They had their big speakers outside dancing to Cash Money songs or New Orleans based artists. All you heard throughout the projects was "Get it ready, get it ready, get it ready, ready. Come on! Talk that stuff nah roll with it". I asked the captain of the team if I could join. She said she would have to think about it. Every project and hood had their own dance team. I just wanted to be down. I watched them practice again a few days later. A few of the girls on the dance team told me I couldn't be on the team. I asked them why and you wouldn't believe their response. They said, "Payless shoes ain't got no grip. They make you fall and bust yo' lip". They busted out laughing and walked away. I liked my shoes. I mean, I'm not understanding how people in the projects could afford Jordan's anyway. Either way it goes, I liked my high top no name brand shoes. My dreams of being on the dance team were shattered. I still taunted them and copied their moves.

I went back to the apartment to tell my mom what happened with the dance team, and it smelled like dead skunks in there. I knew Ms. Kendra and my momma smoked weed, but they started acting like the people from the movie "Crooklyn". I'm referring to the part when they would breathe into brown paper bags to get high. My new stepdad stopped coming around. They must've broken up. Probably because she was going out so much and getting high with Ms. Kendra.

My mom had a new boyfriend named Tyrone that started coming around. His hair was slicked back into a ponytail and he had gold teeth. He was from Baton Rouge. He was cool at first. He didn't really pay any attention to me and my sister. He eventually tried to bond with us, but next thing you know, Ms. Kendra and my mom were gone. They left me, my sister and Megan in the apartment by ourselves for about 2 weeks straight. I was in there making eggs & rice to feed us. We even had rice, butter and sugar. As time went on, we'd eaten all the snacks and food that was left, so we were hungry for at least 2 days. Thank God, Ms. Kendra's mother came knocking one day. She was furious that we were left there alone for that amount of time. She was only going to take Megan, but she decided to take us too. She kept us in a back room in her home. We didn't see Megan. We had to stay in that room, and she would bring us food and drinks. I overheard other voices saying that she shouldn't keep us. I didn't know my grandmother's number, but I knew where she lived. I kept thinking to myself, if I could just show them where she lives, I know she would take us. Within 3 days of staying in that room, my grandmother and grandfather came for us. I don't know how they knew we were there, but we grabbed our jackets and ran to my grandfather's car. My grandmother hugged us and told us to get in the car. They pampered us when we got to their house. My grandfather brought us happy meals from Burger King. My grandmother took us to Stage, the department store, to get some clothes. She worked for the Chamber of Commerce. She had a good job. She was the only black woman working there, and her face was the first face you saw when you walked in. She was the secretary. She walked to and from work Monday through Friday.

After a while, my mom finally came back. She met us at my grandparents' house. My grandmother never kept us away from her, so we left with her again. This time we landed ourselves at a motel called "Kajun Inn". It's right next to McDonald's and a laundry mat. It was a roach motel. It was very disgusting. The pool didn't have any water in it. It just had bugs and lawn chairs thrown in it. I would sit on the steps and watch women get in trucks with men. I watched different men go in and out of this one lady's room. I wasn't slow so I knew she was a prostitute. My heart broke for her. She was a skinny, white woman with blonde hair. I imagined her family coming to get her and giving her a make-over and a better life. I know when my hair is done and I'm dressed pretty, I always feel better. That might not have been enough for her. I thought maybe she just didn't feel pretty enough. Anyway, my mom was still with her new boyfriend Tyrone. He would spend nights at the motel too. It seemed to me that he didn't care about the fact that she had children. I would always bump heads with him. To me, it felt like he wanted my mom all to himself. He never played with us. He just wanted to be under her. When he came over, we had to go play outside and wait until they were finished "talking". I knew they were doing the nasty though. We stayed there for a while. We barely had food. We had no home cooked meals. We just survived off of snacks. We had to eat cereal and water because the milk was always spoiling.

We were on the move again. It was like we were always moving without a plan, like a ship without a sail. We were just moving without any direction. Just being with my mom made it all worth it though. I know some children become resentful, but I loved my mom so much that it didn't matter what she did or didn't do. I just needed her presence. We found ourselves back with my grandparents when they found out we were living at Kajun Inn. One day, my sister, my mom and I were running across the street to go to the gas station by the motel and my grandmother and grandfather saw us. My grandfather blew his horn and pulled over to the side of the street. They took me and my sister back with them. We stayed with them for a few months. It appeared as if my mom was getting herself together, so my grandmother let us go with her yet again. This time, we stayed with Ms. Janice and her husband Dudley. They were a loving couple. Ms. Janice was a minister. She reminded me of Juanita Bynum. She was bold and strong. That's how I met my next childhood friend. Melanie was half African. She was a tomboy that loved to play basketball, and she had a beautiful voice. My mom and her mom did ministry work together. They had a big house right by the Westend Park. We could literally walk to the park from their house. They were kind to us, and Melanie became my best friend. I had to sneak on the bus to get dropped off to their house. I know I was normally supposed to walk to my grandmother's. My little sister and I would hop on the bus and get dropped off at the corner near Ms. Janice's house. We hadn't seen my mom for a few weeks. Ms. Janice and her husband tried everything to make us comfortable. I could see the worry in their faces though. Abandonment never feels good. I wondered if my mom just didn't want to have children. Maybe it was too hard for her. My heart always sympathized with her, even though I was going through my own pain. I always felt bad for her. She left us again. This time for good. I'm turning the combination on my padlock again. My grandmother picked us up for good this time. Now my mom was on drugs full blown and had gotten herself arrested. She was in the Iberia Parish jail. My grandmother had some connections, so she didn't stay there long. When she got out, she didn't stay home with us. She was always on the go. If I wasn't getting teased before, I hadn't seen anything yet! Some of the drug dealers that went to school with me teased me about my mom's addiction. Not all of them, but a few of them did. They would tell me that they had sex with my mom for drugs. I know you're probably thinking "drug dealers in elementary school?". Yes! They were just in a few grades higher than I was, but they were baby gangsters. They were some of the smartest guys I knew. They would fight and get kicked out of school, but I knew it was what the environment had given them. They would tell me that they ran a train on my momma and wanted to know if they could do the same to me. A "train" is when one woman has sex with more than one man, while they all watch in the same room. A part of me believed them and a part of me didn't. I dreaded going to school each day, but having Mya, Kate, Kerri, Brittany and my best friend Cliff, made it easier for me. I wanted my own identity apart from my mom's. I wish they would've gotten to know me, instead of teasing me because of who my mom is. I hadn't seen my mom in weeks. She showed up and disappeared again. When I did see her, I noticed she'd cut all her beautiful hair off. She had a bald fade, and she had lost a lot of weight. There were rumors that my mom was put on drugs by her friend Kendra. I lived in the projects. It was like headline news. All of my friends would tell me what was being said, but my friend Kirsten would always tell me not to worry about it. Her mom was battling with the same addiction and just like mine, her grandmother, Ms. Carolyn took care of her and her siblings. She was such a sweet woman.

My grandmother's friend lived in our neighborhood, Ms. Linda. If no one was home after school, my sister and I would stay there and do our homework until my grandmother got home from work at 5. She had 2 daughters and a son, Shanaya, Marsha and James. They took good care of us. Her daughters were older than us. Her oldest daughter was a Janet Jackson fanatic. That's where I found my love for music outside of our culture. Growing up in the projects, we normally listened to "Cash Money Records taking over for the '99 and 2000" all day, Ya'll. She enjoyed different genres and would have singing contests with us. I would never win, even though I always thought I could sing. I had a huge crush on James. He was the skinniest thing with the biggest ears ever. His two front teeth crossed over each other, but he showed me attention. He was sweet to me. He wanted to do nasty things with me with our clothes on. I would always ask to spend the night there so we could do nasty things together. We got caught a few times and his mom whipped us with a belt. She wouldn't tell my grandmother, but she would tear us both up. She made sure we knew that it wasn't ok for us to be doing that. If you know Ms. Linda, she wasn't someone to play with. She played sports as a teenager. Those butt whippings were every bit of painful. You hear me?! His sister, Marsha kept our hair up with crochet braids or braids to the scalp. She braided tight like the Africans. I never got my hair braided by an African, but I could just about imagine. James was nice to me in private, but he would tease me when the other kids were around. That created another wound.

We had a big tree on the side of our apartment in the projects. I would sit under that tree often to reflect on what was going on in my life. I used one of my extra school notebooks to write poetry about how I was feeling. That cycle with James set the tone for other people to secretly care for me privately and be ashamed of me publicly. That opened the door for my self-worth to decrease. We were kids. We didn't realize how much our actions could impact us later. He was just being a kid. I was just being a kid with issues and a broken heart. If I would tell someone he was my boyfriend, he would say I was lying, confront me and fuss with me in front of them. I kept "dry humping" with him in secret though. He would tell me to keep things between me and him and that people shouldn't be in our business. I laugh at it now because we were so young. How did we even understand those principles? Adults do that now. They put themselves in "situationships". They do things as a couple in private, but it's on the down low publicly. No commitment, no titles, just sex and conversation. We don't realize how much our childhood can impact our adulthood.

I still wasn't convinced that my mom was on drugs, but I should've known from what she did me for Halloween one year. My grandmother had already said we would sit on the porch and pass out candy, but I wanted to get dressed up like the rest of my friends. My mom popped up right on time. She had costumes for me and my sister. We were going to dress up as clowns. She got my sister the red Afro wig and she got me a long blonde wig. She said there weren't any more red wigs left in the store. We got dressed to go trick or treating and my mom did our make-up. I didn't have the red nose either, but she put some black lip liner around my lips with red lipstick. My body was overly developed for my age. I had breasts, but they weren't that big. They were shaped like elbows, but I had some. I had hips and my butt was a little plump. Ya'll know clowns wear jumpsuits. Mine was tight and I had my white high-top shoes on. My mom took us trick or treating in every hood and project. We even went to a project called Dodge City. It looks just like Cedar Hill, the projects that we lived in at the time. We lived in Dodge City for a short period of time when I was a little girl, also. We get back there and here I am knocking on people's doors asking for candy. These 2 gay men, Paul and Harlan, were standing by a house next to the projects. They asked me what I was dressed as. Before I could tell them who I was, Harlan said, "Come on nah that child dressed up like Lil' Kim". The other said, "Her momma wrong for that" and they laughed at me. I would've laughed too. Shucks! My momma was wrong for that. That blonde wig and lip liner did enough. I was always happy with her no matter what she did. She even paid for me and my friend Kirsten to go see "Austin Powers Gold Member" at the movies. She tried her best, despite her addiction. The only hard part is that I longed for her. I wanted to be with her. It didn't matter how much my grandparents would spoil us. I just wanted my mom. I felt so alone without her. She made me laugh. It never really matters what your parents do. The undying love you have for them is irreplaceable and irrevocable. I just wanted to see her smile. I needed and wanted a hug or something. I just wanted her to comb my hair, play a board game, watch a movie, bake a cake or something that mothers and daughters do together.

Chapter 5

To put the icing on the cake, my mom found herself in jail again. This time, it was for prostitution. We would go visit her every Saturday. That was my first time ever going to a jail. They pat you down, you have to sign in and tell them who you're there to see. This time my grandmother was unable to use the pull she had with the people at the courthouse because my mom kept getting into trouble. Every time I asked my grandparents why they haven't gone to get my mom yet, they would say because her bond was too high. I missed her! She was the only person that I could talk to that understood me. She was one of those moms that made you feel comfortable enough to express yourself. The only thing I dreaded about going to see her, was the fact that she would make us model for the other women in jail. Showing off our outfits. My grandmother had a passion for fashion, and it has trickled down on to me. So, we were always dressed nice when we went to visit her.

After everything that happened with my stepdad, I saw she was trying to take a better approach with us. Until drugs and the streets took her away. We all need our mother's love. Not having it can weigh on you. I had no help channeling all the feelings I had. I didn't even know how to express them, except to write in my notebook. I would make up poems and write stories. I just wanted to be accepted and loved. I felt if people would dig beyond the surface, they would find me. I'm turning the combination to my padlock again. I don't know about you, but I have a lot of numbers on my padlock. It's so many experiences I've had that began to turn my heart cold. Things were happening back to back and my behavior reflected it. I'm 10 years old now, getting suspended from school. I can't even think of a reason why my grandmother let him back in our lives. I think it's because my mom was in jail, and he was helping her financially. He would also buy us shoes, clothes, bikes and toys just like he did when we were family. He had a new wife now. They lived in St. Martinville, another little city down the way. We didn't just visit with him for a day. We visited with him for the whole weekend and sometimes on school breaks. It pains me to say that I was getting abused again. It was the same thing when he was with my mom. His new wife worked nights. She had a son and a daughter from a previous relationship, but they didn't have children together at this point. As soon as she would leave for work, he would come get me out of bed. By this time, my body was more developed than the last time we saw him. He even had the nerve to tell me I was shaped like my mom. He told me how sexy I was and how fine I was. I tried to fight him this time around. He'd put on the pornographic movies, and

I would keep my eyes closed. He would whip me with a belt and tell me to open my eyes. He took the dining room table chairs and grabbed some rope. He put duct tape on my mouth and tied each hand and leg to a different chair. Each time, he tried to get inside of me, and each time he would get inside of me more and more. He reached his goal, eventually. The pain was unbearable. I was bleeding and crying. The restraints were so tight and every time I tried to move, it would get tighter. After he finished, he wiped himself off with a towel and untied me. He didn't take the tape off, and he tied my hands together. He put me in the bathtub and told me that he popped my cherry and that's why I was bleeding. He said, "You're a woman now". He proceeded to say, "You're my girlfriend now". All I could do was cry. He washed me off and told me I needed to soak in the tub a little while before getting out. My innocence was stolen from me. No matter what I've been through, I've always tried to make the best out of my situations and have joy. At that very moment, I felt like life wasn't worth living. I wanted to be dead. I felt so unloved and weak. How could I let him do this to me again? Why didn't I fight harder? He would have his way with me, and I had no help. He would make me perform sexual acts on him. He would perform sexual acts on me. It was never pleasurable for me. I was a child. He would suck on my breast and compliment my body parts as he touched me. If I didn't cry, he would go harder to make me cry. For some strange reason, seeing me cry did something for him. It's like it turned him on to see me cry and struggle. He instilled so much fear inside of me. Every weekend I dreaded packing my bag. It got to the point to where I wouldn't even cry anymore. I would just let him do whatever he wanted to do to me. I got tired of fighting and being beaten. I was tired of struggling. I felt empty inside, and I just didn't care anymore. I would lay there, and it didn't matter how much it hurt. I would not let him see me cry.

The best part about coming back home was being on the dance team. Yes, Ya'll! I'm finally on a dance team. I watched them practice all the time. My grandmother wouldn't let me join and I didn't have rhythm, but I watched them and learned all their moves. There were girls from other hoods on the team. That's how good they were. Everybody wanted to be a "Cedar Hill Dream Girl". That was the name of our group. The captain of the team was Lashae. Her mom, Ms. Anita, did hair and sponsored the team. We did fundraisers to pay for our uniforms for the parades. We had royal blue shorts and white t-shirts with our names on the back. We wore white Ked tennis shoes with little pom-poms on them. My shirt had "Nunny" on the back of it. They put me to the back of the line with Jeremiah and James. Jeremiah was James's best friend. He danced really good too. The only reason I was on the team was because someone dropped out, and I knew all of their moves. They were shocked because I got up and instantly fell in line. They had to work with me on my rhythm, but I did whatever they needed me to do. My girls Phaedra and

Kirsten would have practices with me on the side to help me. I told them what my stepdad had been doing to me. They said that I should tell someone. I knew my family wouldn't listen because they didn't listen the first time I'd told them. I had a talk with God. I talked to Him a lot, but I never really heard Him say anything back to me.

I grew up in the church most of my childhood. My mom was a full, blown rider for God. She was connected to so many women of God. One of them owned a daycare. Her name was Ms. Betty Lee. She had a daycare center with a bus that picked us up when I was too young to attend school. Her daughters were teachers at the daycare. They each taught different age groups. I was always drawn to Ms. KeKe and Ms. Daisy. Ms. Daisy was fine as wine. She had big hips and a little waist. Well, really all of her daughters were shaped like that. You know that old saying, "She get it from her momma"? They would even take us on little vacations and trips. She had children from every hood and project there. A lot of the kids' mothers didn't have family to depend on and couldn't afford other options, so Ms. Betty was a blessing to so many. She taught us how to pray and let us listen to gospel music. The only part I didn't like was nap time. The cots were so hard. I hated lunch time, also. Only because we were forced to eat beets. I know a lot of people like beets, but I think God shouldn't have created that vegetable. It's just nasty. They made sure you ate all of your food. I had to hold my nose to swallow the beets.

The seeds that were planted in me stuck with me, and God would send people to water them along the way. When a seed comes to rest in its appropriate place with conditions suitable to its germination, it breaks open. I never found a suitable condition to break out. I was always in the dark under the dirt. My conversation with God was one simple word, "Help". I asked Him to rescue me. That Monday at school, I went to the guidance counselor's office, and I told the school counselor that I was being molested. She made me tell her every detail. She gave me a cup of water and something to color, as I talked to her about it. After I stayed with her for a few hours, her eyes began to fill with tears, and she sent me back to class. I knew she was going to call my grandmother. I was so scared at school. In the black community we have this "whatever happens in this house stays in this house" policy. It's like putting other people in the family's business, and it doesn't matter how bad it is, you weren't supposed to tell anyone. When I got home my grandmother was still at work. I thought if I went to sleep early my grandmother wouldn't ask me anything. When she got home, she came in my room and asked me if it was true. I told her yes. She hugged me and told me that I didn't have to go there anymore. I felt so relieved and happy. She didn't call the cops or anything and nothing happened to him. He was still in the clear. I wanted him to get in trouble. I wanted someone to beat him up or something. However, I was satisfied with not having to go to his house anymore.

I was even more happy when my mom was released from jail. She did the back and forth thing with seeing us. I know she was on drugs, but she was so fun. We would see my mom all the time by my Aunt Marie's house. My grandmother would let us go spend weekends at my Aunt Marie's house. Aunt Marie was my favorite aunt. She would get drunk, smoke her cigarettes and listen to old school music. She turned me on to Earth, Wind and Fire and Frankie Beverly and Maze. I loved "Happy Feelings". She always cooked for us and let us play outside until we passed out. She was the best person in the world to me. She cursed you out and still made you feel loved. My mom visited her all the time, so we would see her often. My aunt lived in an area that had a lot of drug dealers and drug users. People criticize and have their feelings about people who are addicted to drugs, but they have some of the best personalities.

My mom had very interesting friends. She had a gay friend named Rico. He would put finger waves in my hair. I always had an old soul. People didn't understand it though. I got teased for wearing my finger waves. Rico was so funny and always had an attitude. He looked a lot like Waymon from the movie, "Low Down Dirty Shame". Getting my hair done was always time well spent with my mom. Any time spent with her was great.

My friend Shelly lived right across the street from my Aunt Marie's house. I would walk over to her house after getting my hair done by Rico. He would do my hair at my Aunt Marie's house. Her mom and my mom were good friends before she started using drugs. Ms. Georgia brought me and my sister our first and only pair of Jordan's. She always dressed nice, and she kept her children matching her fly. Shelly and her older sister Chanel had all the latest shoes and clothing.

Their mom was always so neat, and she liked nice things. It was nice of her to bless us with some new shoes. Shelly and I became friends when she lived in the same projects as we did. She had a Barbie tent and we played inside of it most of the time. We would even take sheets and throw it over the clothes lines to make a tent and pretend it was a house. In the projects, our backyards were filled with little white flowers. I couldn't tell you what they were called, but we pulled them up and made necklaces and rings with them. We thought that was so much fun.

One day when Shelly and her family still lived in the projects, we were playing outside, and a little girl named Evette spotted us. She had red hair and a dusty brown complexion. She was a tomboy and acted a lot like our age group version of Debo from the movie, "Friday". We were all scared of her. She saw us playing and told us to come see. That means she called us over. She said her grandmother had all the doors locked, and she needed to do the "number 2". She asked us to stand in front of her to hide her while she poo'd. Shelly and I both said no, but she told us she would slap the spit out of our mouth, so we did it. She squatted down by a tree and we turned our backs to her. She told us to face her and turn our backs the other way. She literally made us watch her poop and made me hand her a big leaf to wipe her butt with. I'm dying laughing because we were really that scared of her that we allowed her punk us into doing that. I missed Shelly after she left the projects, but I was glad she lived across the street from my aunt. Every weekend, I made my way to my aunt's house to see Shelly.

I was still acting out at school though. I told one of my classmates that I had an imaginary friend named Elf and he was bi-sexual. I told him Elf liked him and wanted to go out with him. He told the teacher on me. Everybody always snitched on me. I got suspended from school, and I was banned from going to my aunt's house for the weekend. My grandmother made me write the word bi-sexual on a piece of paper 500 times. We had a bush in our front yard. She made me go get a "switch" from the bush. A "switch" is what we called a small branch from a tree or bush. I took my time taking the leaves off of it trying to avoid a whipping. I heard a voice by the screen door yell, "If you don't hurry up with them damn leaves, before I beat yo' ass with the whole tree". She startled me and I jumped. Man, it felt like she was the Incredible Hulk after she finished wearing me out. I never said the word bi-sexual again.

So, I decided, because I needed some attention, to make up stories that I was having sex. Lord knows I wasn't, but I thought that was the down thing to do. I wasn't having sex at all, but I would make up names of guys that supposedly snuck in my window at night. I talked about how we had these wild passionate sex sessions. I just wanted to be down, but guess what I did? I created a reputation for myself that added to my plate of being bullied. Now, I was called freak and hoe all off of lies. Again, sitting under the magnolia tree, crumbling leaves in my hands and watching the wind take them away. I became the target of boys wanting to have sex with me and not just make-believe sex. One of the gangsters from elementary school that I mentioned previously, came to the projects and told me how much he liked me. It's a shame how boys know how to finesse girls at such a young age. He was just trying to have sex with me. He was really cute. All the girls liked him. He was stocky and his hair was thick and wavy. I couldn't believe he liked me. He kept asking me to take him inside of my house. My grandmother was at work and no one was home, so I thought it would be a good idea. That good idea turned into the worst idea ever. This was the first time I'd ever done something like this. Even though I made up stories about being sexually active, I really wasn't. At that time, the closest I'd gotten to having sex willingly was dry humping with my neighbor. He pulled his pants down and told me to sit on it. I tried, but it wouldn't go in. Next thing I knew, I heard voices in the living room. My aunt had come back home with her friend Saunya. We jumped up, pulled up our pants and sat on side of each other on the bed. In the apartments we lived in, the closets didn't have doors. It was just a big opening with shelves, so he couldn't hide in the closet. My bed was really low, and he was big and tall. He couldn't fit under there either. My aunt walked in the room. She immediately started fighting the boy. She could fight really good. She was beating him like he'd stolen something. She beat him all the way out of the back door. I sat on the bed and cried because I knew I was next. She beat me like I was a grown woman. She kneed me in my face, slapped and punched me. She didn't stop until her friend tried to get her off of me. At this point, I was bleeding. She was yelling at me, "You want to be a lil' hoe. So, you fucking now?". I kept saying no, we didn't do anything. She beat me so bad I had to take pain meds, and I slept half the day away. I was so ashamed and embarrassed. I felt like dying because everybody in the projects knew what happened, and I knew he was going to go to school and tell everybody, as well. My grandfather came in the room that night to check on me. He was so patient and kind to me. He said, "How long have you been doing things like this?" I told him it was my first time and that I was sorry. He told me he would see about getting me on birth control. He was disappointed in me, but he forgave me and told me to never let it happen again. He told me I was beautiful and that he loved me. He walked out and closed the door behind him. My grandmother kept me home from school for a couple of days so that the smoke could clear. I had so much on my mind. It's not a good feeling to be a child and not understand what you're going through. I can admit that I didn't. I had no one to talk to. My mom was on drugs and even though my dad took a paternity test to prove to himself that I was his, he still wasn't in the picture. I saw him once a year, if that. I would see him randomly at parades or events.

My dad's side of the family, whom I look like more than my mom's side, would try to build a relationship with me. My aunts had no idea about the abuse I was going through and when I was with them, I just wanted to enjoy those bonding moments. I got to see and spend time with beautiful women who looked like me. They were very neat and well put together. They were always shopping and buying me little gifts when they saw me. I still had no one around me who understood how low my self-esteem had gotten. I was broken at such a young age. The old folks used to say, "You better enjoy being a child because when you become an adult, you're going to wish you were still a child". I just wanted to fast forward my life into adulthood. Childhood just wasn't working out for me. I blamed myself for everything. What if I wouldn't have told my mom that my stepdad was molesting me? Maybe she wouldn't be on drugs, and we could all still be together. As the days went by, I felt more and more empty inside. I thought telling jokes and being the class clown made people like me. I thought it took away from the fact that my mom was on drugs, and I was labeled as a nasty freak. So, I told jokes. I was very disruptive in class. I even teased other people. Hurt people really do hurt people. I was living proof. When we don't heal properly, it becomes a vicious cycle of people hurting each other. I pretended to be ok. I wanted acceptance from the very people that were hurting me. We can become the very thing that we despise, if we try to treat others the way they treat us. I knew how it felt to be bullied. I should've known better. I had no idea of the magnitude of what I was doing. I was bleeding on others and causing them to bleed. Words are powerful. They cut deep and penetrate your soul if you're not strong enough to shield yourself from them.

Chapter 6

I would tell jokes about my grandfather cheating on my grandmother. I was a natural. I had this one joke where I said, "My grandfather is cheating on my grandmother. She told him if he got caught cheating again, she was going to leave him. Well one day she got home from work, and he was in there having sex with a midget. My grandmother said, 'How could you do this to me? I'm leaving!'. My grandfather stood in front of her and said, 'Please baby, don't leave me! Can't you see I'm trying to cut back!'. Get it? Don't laugh too hard and drop this book! He said he was cutting back because it's a midget. I was a mess. That was the only way I felt something, by making people laugh. We even remixed Deborah Cox's song. "How did you get here? (Bitch, I caught the bus.) Nobody supposed to be here. (I just want to fuck.) I've tried that love thing for the last time. My heart says no, no. (Bitch, your heart can't talk.) If you didn't sing this in school, you weren't cool. My sense of humor didn't do me any justice because I stayed in the principal's office. I would catch whippings at home, be good for a little while and do it all again.

When I stepped into puberty, I showed my friends that I had pubic hair, in the school restroom. I told them I rubbed butter on my chest to make my breasts grow. I was probably the youngest girl in my classes, but the most physically developed. I had everything, except hair on my head. I was bald-headed and bad. I should've picked a struggle. We all handle things in different ways. What I went through caused me to act out and no one thought, "Well maybe we should get her some counseling". Black folk never want to seek outside help. If you're having mental issues, they just write you off as crazy. Nobody ever gets to the root of the problem. No one ever asks "Why?". We just move on with our lives and stay away from people who cause discomfort in our perfect world. We never get to the root of the issue or seek help. Some people say it's not their business, but what are we put on this earth for? I had to throw all of that into my closet, lock my padlock and get ready for the most wonderful time of the year.

The best part of the year was here and that's Christmas. My grandparents would take us riding to see all the houses with lights. They always got us hot chocolate and cookies for the ride. We would listen to old school Christmas songs. We listened to the Temptations "Silent Night". I loved when the singer with the deep voice would say ""T'was the night before Christmas". We listened to Nat King Cole's "Chestnuts". The Jackson 5's "Santa Claus is Coming to Town" was one of my favorites. In class, we wrote letters to Santa and colored sheets of paper with

Christmas ornaments on them. I told my friends all the things I added to my list to Santa. A boy named Jordan said out loud, in front of the whole class, "I don't know what Shalara's writing a letter to Santa Claus for". Ya'll don't have chimneys in the projects". Everybody busted out laughing. I laughed too, to make it seem like I didn't care. Deep down, I wanted to bust him in his mouth. I wasn't letting him steal my Christmas joy. Christmas is my favorite holiday.

You're not from Louisiana if you've never heard "A Cajun Night Before Christmas". Santa had a boat and some alligators. That's some Cajun stuff right there, for real. My grandfather would buy us a real Christmas tree every year, and we would all decorate it together. He would pop popcorn, take a needle and thread and put the popcorn on the thread. We wrapped it around the Christmas tree like garland. That was our Christmas tradition. We would light up the tree, but not for a long time because my grandmother would always complain about her light bill being too high. We baked cookies for Santa on the night before Christmas. One night, I walked all around the house to see if we had a chimney. The only thing I saw were vents. I asked my grandfather how Santa Claus would get in to bring presents. He said, he would get in through the back door. I didn't believe him. I asked my friend Miriam if Santa came through their back door. She told me Santa wasn't real and her parents buy her everything. I felt like my life flashed before my eyes. I didn't care what she said. I still believed.

I needed to believe that the world had some magic in it. Every day, I would wake up and go play with Miriam. She was the coolest. She was one of my best friends. Her dad had gotten into a bad car accident, so his stance and positioning were different from others. The other kids would say mean things about her dad's condition, but I never did. I thought it was cool that he still functioned and took care of his family the way he did. I always wanted to spend the night at her house, but her mom would always tell me no. She would say, "Oh no baby! I have a son". I always pouted when she said that. Thank God for her wisdom. So many young girls get hurt due to irresponsible adults. Now that I'm older, I couldn't thank her and love her enough for that.

My family received a great blessing on January 21, 1999. My second little sister was born. Remember the guy my mom was dating when we lived at the motel? Well, she had a beautiful baby girl for him. She was born in Baton Rouge, La. His mom had taken them in to help them get on their feet. I hadn't met my new sister yet. My grandfather got us up one morning and said let's go on a road trip. He took us to see my baby sister. I was named after my aunt. My sister Allison was named after her dad. When they told me my new sister's name, the comedian in me could not be contained. They named her Sunsiouxra. We were told it means "Sunshine" in Indian dialect. Naming her Sunshine would have been just fine. They could've even named her Sunflower Seed. I just couldn't believe she named that baby

Sunsiouxra. It sounded like an expensive dish at a high-end restaurant. My poor sister Allison couldn't pronounce it. She said, "What's her name? Some Sausage?". Black people swear that they have Indian in their blood just because their cheekbones are high, and they have good hair. Their great grandmother was an Indian. Now, in some cases, that's true, but we definitely know how to exaggerate. Just like everybody in New Iberia says they're related to Beyoncé. The whole New Iberia is Beyoncé's cousins.

My new baby sister was so beautiful. She was so tiny. She looked a lot like my mom. She had her nose and the shape of her lips. A lot of people say that I look like my mom, but I have a lot of my dad family's facial features. We didn't see my little sister again until she was about 8 months old. She came to live with us at my grandparents' house. We all took turns spoiling her. Just like when I was a baby, she didn't have much hair. We gave her a nick name. It was "Mostanky". Weird right? I know! We all have jacked up nick names in the black community. I have never heard of a white person having a nick name. If they do, it's very rare and subtle.

As a child, I would watch a cartoon called "Rolie Polie Olie" with my little sister every morning. She looked just like the characters because her face was so round and so was her stomach. We would also watch "The Little Mermaid". That was my favorite cartoon. My grandmother bought me the blanket and the house slippers. I fell in love with the storyline because she desperately wanted to change her circumstances, and just like the Little Mermaid, I just wanted to find my legs. I felt like she felt; stuck in that fish tail and had no space to move. She never gave up though. She even made some mistakes trying to get free. I should've known I was different by the way I dissected everything and gave it a deeper meaning. My mom loves that about me. She would ask me to tell her what songs mean and I would explain what the artist is trying to say. I did that with cartoons and movies, as well. I guess that's why I would constantly watch "To Wong Foo" and "The Color Purple". Each time, I had a different meaning and understanding for it. After being hurt so many times, we take our gifts, put them in a box and place them on a shelf. Pain becomes our new normal, so it's no use in doing things we enjoy. Being who you really want to be, who you know you really are, doesn't seem to work when you're operating out of hurt.

My godmother continued to stretch my mind. She would send me books to read. I would finish them within a day or two. She was in nursing school at the university in Lafayette, and she worked. She was a great role model for me. She knew what my mother was going through. She stepped right in, even in the process of working and studying. She didn't have any children, but she took me on as her responsibility in a way. I would cry not to leave her house. When she moved to Houston, I was devastated. Even though, before she left, her long-term boyfriend and now husband, teased me for getting beat up. Yes, that's right. Kerri, my friend who I teased from time to time, grabbed me by the hood of my jacket and spun me around. She released the hood, and I flew into a big mound of dirt on the playground at school. She didn't get suspended, but I did because I teased her. She was about to fight with Kate, and I started singing, "A fight, a fight, a skinny and a fat". Of course, everyone laughed. I guess she had it bottled up from all the other times I teased her. Next thing I knew I'm spinning in the air. My eye was swollen, my lip was busted, and my left cheek had a big gash on it. No one was concerned about my medical needs because I had a reputation of being a misfit. I was even suspended. I had to spend those days with my nanny and her boyfriend. They were still living in Louisiana at the time. The good part was that they had a pool, so it was like I was on a mini vacation. She owned books on top of books. I enjoyed reading, but my teachers would never know that because of my bad behavior. I sacrificed so much because of that.

So, my godmother moved to Houston, but nonetheless, she would send me bus tickets to go spend time with her. My cousin Anna and I would always go back and forth. We would come back home with so much stuff. That's right! My nanny became a nurse. That didn't stop her schooling. She had so much ambition and drive, and she came from the same projects as I did. I know we could easily become the product of our environments, but sometimes people have a different reaction to the environment. They grow different. They do the total opposite of what's presented to them. They want better.

They are determined to rise above their circumstances to create a better life. They change the climate of their environment so that they can grow productively. We all have this superpower, but some of us haven't tapped into it because our pain and abuse have created a wall. Nothing positive, nothing that gives life and light can permeate the wall you've put up. You can't break those barriers until you realize they exist. It's become normal for us to feel pain. It's normal for us to hurt and be misunderstood and mistreated. So, we start a never-ending cycle of hurt people, hurting people. I imagined more for myself, but I didn't quite know how to turn my dreams into reality. I had no idea that faith plus works equals manifestation. I had no idea that if I cooperated with God, all things would work out for my good. My pain and anguish didn't allow me to see God, even when he used people to show me His love. Those seeds were just piling up. They never dissolved nor did the wind blow them away as the crumbled leaves did. They were just sitting there on the inside of me lying dormant.

I created quite a reputation for myself. People would tell me, "Your name is ringing", and that never was a good thing to hear. It meant that your name was ringing in the streets. People were talking about you. Things were about to get worse for me. I know you're probably thinking can it get any worse than it's already been. Yes, unfortunately, it does. My friend Kirsten and I would go walking with my mom sometimes. That was the cool thing to do back then. Walking uptown was the highlight of our weekend. My mom was still on drugs, but she was fun to be around. She would get us anything we wanted. She never let anyone touch or harm us. Kirsten and I would get dressed in our flyest gear to go walking with her. I was 10 years old, but I was over-developed for my age. I looked like I could've been a teenager. Drug dealers hanging on the block would ask her to hook them up with me. She would say she's "Jail Bait". That meant that I was too young to talk to, and they could go to jail for dealing with me. She would also threaten them if they ever tried anything.

One night, I was missing my mom. I hadn't seen her in a few weeks. The last time I'd seen her, she was losing more and more weight. I don't know what I was thinking, but I snuck out of the house to go look for her. I waited until I knew my grandparents were asleep, and I snuck out of the back door. I walked from the projects all the way to a street that I knew she frequented. It had to be after midnight. I saw a group of guys sitting on a porch, and I asked them if they had seen my mom. One of them told me that she was in a house across the street from where we were. He said he could take me to her. I followed him. I knew my mom would be upset that I snuck out of the house, but I needed to see her and make sure she was ok. It was very dark in the house, and it looked abandoned. I didn't think that she wasn't in there because I know that's where most drug addicts hung out. He walked me through a hallway, opened a door, guided me inside and closed the door behind me while saying, "She's probably in here". I was scared and nervous. It was so dark. I couldn't see anything. I waited for a moment. After not hearing anything, I turned to feel for the door so that I could leave. Clearly my mom or anyone, for that matter, was in the room or in the house. I felt myself being pulled on as I was trying to make my way out. I heard voices saying, "Where do you think you're going". I asked them to please let me leave. I heard so many different voices and so much laughter. I felt hands touching my legs and abdominal area. I tried to tell them I was only 10 years old, but they didn't believe me. I screamed my mom's name, and that's when someone grabbed my mouth from behind and threw me on a mattress. I had on white shorts and the Valentine's Day edition Nikes that my cousin Anna let me borrow. I knew she was going to kill me for wearing them again. They were way too big for my feet, but I wanted to wear them so bad. They took off my shoes and pulled off my shorts. One person was holding my right wrist down, another the other wrist, and the same for my ankles. The person that got on top of me put their hand over my mouth. He put himself inside of me and told me to stop fighting. He moaned and grunted as I cried and tried to get up. They each took time getting on top of me. They were laughing and saying that I wanted it because I left the house at that time of the night. I cried and laid there for what felt like hours. I begged them to stop. I pleaded with them to let me go. Eventually, they let me get up, but more men walked in and asked where I was going. I tried to run past them, but one of them picked me up and threw me back on the mattress. It seemed as if they called people and told them I was there. I didn't understand why this was happening to me. I was so confused. The little bit of light I had left inside of me was shattered completely in that moment. They kept me there for over 4 hours. After they finished, someone handed me my clothes. I put my shorts and shoes on and ran out of that house as fast as I could. My legs were sore. I had blood running down my legs. My white shorts were full of it. Seems like I ran the whole way home. I was scared and crying, afraid that they would follow me home and take me back to that house. I snuck back into the house. When I looked at the clock, it was a little after 5 AM. I took off my shorts, put them in a grocery bag and threw them away in our big garbage bend outside. I ran some cold water on a towel and washed my body off. It hurt so bad to use the bathroom. I washed my face, put on my night gown and got in the bed. I cried myself to sleep.

I had a friend named Lillian. We bonded from my neighbors babysitting us. She also lived next door to my Aunt Marie. We talked on the phone all the time. She lived in the area where it all happened. I told her what they did to me. I cried to her, and I made her promise not to tell anyone. I was so afraid of getting in trouble for sneaking out of the house. I wasn't thinking clearly about the severity of what I'd just experienced. Even at her young age, she knew what happened to me wasn't ok. She cried with me on the phone. She saw my mom walking down her street shortly after we hung up the phone. My mom frequented the street she lived on. She told my mom everything that happened to me. Later that day, my mom came storming through the door to tell my grandmother what happened. She was crying and angry. She asked me why I'd left the house at that time of the night. She said, "Under no circumstances are you to come looking for me". She paced back and forth, saying how she was going to kill them. My grandmother told her to take me to the police station to make a report before she gets herself into trouble. We walked to the police station together. As we walked, she kept asking me the names of the guys who did it to me. I only knew a few of them. The others, I didn't know. I only remembered the guys I saw sitting on the porch when I first got there, but there were more guys that came afterwards. When we got into the police station, she told the police officer at the window that she needed to report a rape. Two officers took us into a room to take our statement. They began to question me about what happened. I told them the complete truth. I told them that I snuck out of the house because I missed my mom and wanted to see her. I could tell the questions were making my mom uncomfortable. The police didn't seem to care about her discomfort. They asked me how many men were present. I told them it was dark, but from the voices and how long they kept me there, I estimated that it was over 20 guys. I gave them the names of the guys that I knew, but I couldn't tell them who else was in the room. I kept my head down as I talked because I was so embarrassed and ashamed. I was scared that the police would think I consented to it. I really didn't believe that people could get in trouble for sexual abuse of a child because my stepdad was never punished.

Spring

Nature is reborn in this season.

Deuteronomy 11:14 says, "That I will give you the rain of your land in his due season, the first rain and the latter rain, that thou mayest gather in thy corn, and thy wine, and thine oil." (KJV) In order for the harvest to be ready, the rain has to come first. You ever walked through rain? Flowers can't grow without rain. But when it rains, it pours. So, we don't think about the harvest or the flowers. We focus on the rain and become weary.

Chapter 7

I thought men could just take what they wanted, and it was nothing you could do to stop it. It was all I knew from the abuse I'd sustained from men. Seemingly, they got away with abusing me. The officers saw the bruises on my wrists and told my mom that I needed to get a rape kit done at the nearest hospital, and that they would follow us there. Before we got up to leave, they asked me had this happened to me before. Did someone ever touch me inappropriately before this happened? I shook my head "yes". They asked me by whom, and I said my stepdad's name. My mom started to do this jittery thing that drug addicts do. They asked me was it reported. I said no. My mom kind of looked away. One of the police officers looked angry and sad. From the look on his face, I could tell he knew that the adults in my life had failed me. He couldn't believe it. His face turned red like a crawfish. He just kept telling me how sorry he was that I had to go through that. That was the first time anyone had ever told me they were sorry that I had to experience that level of trauma. It was hard for me to turn my padlock. I struggled more with this than anything else.

I remember Aretha Franklin's song "A Rose Is Still a Rose" came on in the taxi, as we rode to the hospital. I looked out of the window and cried. My mom was rocking back and forth and talking about killing the guys who did what they did to me. She was also mad that I mentioned my stepdad's name. She said that made her look bad and that's not what we were there for. As the song was playing in the car, I thought to myself that I couldn't possibly still be a rose. My rose petals were blowing in the wind never knowing where they would land. We made it to the hospital. My mom told me that she wasn't mad at me and to tell them anything they needed to know, so they could do their jobs. That gave me a little relief because she seemed really upset with me. My mom has never liked to be embarrassed. She can't stand it, but I believe that we remain in bondage when we don't admit our truths and when we don't want to face our issues head on. She'll have to go through her combination to unlock her own padlock because I can't do it for her. Likewise, she can't do it for me. All the medical staff looked shocked and sad once the officer explained to them what I was there for. They asked me to get into a hospital gown so they could examine me. When I opened my legs, I heard the doctor gasp. I had severe abrasions on my vaginal area and bruises on my thighs and abdomen. They used a large Q-tip to get samples, and I had to give blood and take a pregnancy test. As we were waiting for the results, they took pictures of my private area and wanted the clothes I had on that night. I told them it was in the trash bend at my grandparents' house, so they sent an officer to go get them. I was so nervous. The nurse must have noticed the nervousness on my face. She said, "You are the bravest 10-year-old I've ever seen. Everything is going to be ok". I wanted to believe that. It sounded good. I wanted to believe that I was brave and that everything was going to be ok. The longer I sat in the room, the more I realized that it was, in fact, going to be ok.

Before this happened, I made plans to start middle school on a fresh page. I wouldn't be the class comedian. I wouldn't fuss and fight with anyone. I would pay attention in class. I was so smart, but I did the bare minimum just because I wanted to be accepted and cool. I wanted to make people laugh instead of having them laugh at me. This incident only pushed me more into the dirt. I had a game plan on how I was going to come out and now I'm ten steps further from where I started. They discharged me. I went home and my grandfather looked so depressed. It was like he couldn't look at me, but he asked me if I was hungry. Of course, I was. I wanted a burger. Without hesitation, he left to go get it. My sister Allison hugged me really tight and asked if I wanted to go play. I said yes. I needed her in that very moment. We put bubbles on the floor and grabbed our skates. We thought that was so much fun. We had to maintain our balance while skating on the bubbles. The project floors were made of concrete. So, if you fell, Lord be with you because it hurts so bad. We played and played and played until it was bath time. Everyone in the house seemed to be walking on eggshells with me. No one was mad that I snuck out of the house. They just wanted to make sure I was ok. My aunt wanted names. She was livid. I thought my aunt was the best fighter in the world. She would fight girls and beat them up. She would even fight men. She didn't care how big or small you were. Just don't stare at her too long and please don't say anything crazy. I told her everything she wanted to know, and she left out of the house. I was hoping she wouldn't get herself in any trouble.

I also thought about my mom. Once we had gotten home, she left again. I didn't want anyone to hurt her because of me. I've seen how these gangsters and drug dealers do women that's on drugs. I definitely didn't want that for my mom. I took a bath and my grandmother gave me Tylenol for pain. I sat in my bed and prayed that the police would find everybody that participated and lock them away, before anyone in my family gets in trouble. I thought about my dad, and I wished he was around. If he would've been there, I would've been ok. He would've been able to protect me. I felt so foolish. Why did I leave the house? Someone could've kidnapped or killed me. Now here I am, crumbling the leaves in my hands and watching the wind take it away. I could barely sit down from the pain. After a few days had passed, my grandmother finally let me go play outside. All my friends wanted to know what happened and if I was ok. They said they heard about it. I told them what happened. They said well we heard they gave your momma drugs to let them have sex with you. I told them that I didn't believe that. They made it seem as if they knew it was true. I never let that sink in because I was not going to believe that about my mom. I was the one that snuck out of the house. She couldn't have known I was going to go looking for her. People make up things and they believe whatever they want. They look for something that makes more sense or sounds better. For a moment, I almost believed it, but I shook it off. I refused to absorb it. I refused to add that to my pile of heartbreaks. They also said that they heard I wanted it.

People find ways to make the victims feel less than and make excuses for the predators. I began to tell them how unfair it was for them to be glorified. I was only 10 years old, and they had no right. The sad part is, I really didn't believe that myself. I felt like the biggest loser in the world. I just couldn't show them that. I couldn't show them that I was weak. None of the knowledge and wisdom I had could protect me from the troubles of this world.

To add insult to injury, as the day went on and I was mingling with my friends, a black car pulls up and rolls the window down. It was the older brother of one of the guys who had assaulted me. He yelled at me and called me all kinds of names. He called me a freak and said I wanted it. I ran through the apartments as fast as I could. I sat on someone's back porch until the sun went down. I sat there and cried my eyes out. One thing I remembered him saying was that I was a rat. I assumed the police must've questioned them or even arrested someone. I was scared. I didn't leave that back porch until I heard my grandmother calling my name to go inside for the day. Humiliation, guilt, abandonment, rejection, and abuse opened the door to my depression. I was still fighting it in my own way by acting out and trying to be a comedian. I was trying to fight it. I really was. I thought I had everything under control. I didn't even tell my grandmother what happened outside. I knew nothing would truly be done about it and I didn't want my family to get hurt. It started to get out of hand. The girlfriends of the guys that hurt me got my number somehow and started calling me. My grandmother would hand me the phone thinking it was one of my friends calling for me. As soon as I would say hello, they would curse me out and tell me to stop lying. One of them even called me a crack baby. One day, one of them called and she simply wanted to know if it was true and if her boyfriend was in the room. My grandmother saw the look on my face and asked what was wrong. I told her who it was on the phone and what she wanted. She grabbed the phone and said, "She's been through enough. Please leave her alone and don't call her anymore". I went to my room. I cried because it had become such a big deal. Everywhere I turned someone wanted to know what happened. My cousin Anna was smart like my nanny. She was in high school when all of this happened. She was in a program called Upward Bound where she took college courses at UL Lafayette. The girlfriends of the guys who molested me would leave her notes on her dorm room door; picking with her. Some of them were in Upward Bound, also. They would question her about it. She almost got into a fight over it. It was spreading like wildfire.

The police didn't even contact us or come back to question me. We hadn't heard anything from them for a long time. The only thing I knew is that it seemed like the world was against me. My grandmother and my godmother thought it would be best for me to go spend time with my godmother in Houston. My cousin and her best friend came out there with me. I just needed a break from all the craziness. It felt good to get away. We went shopping for school uniforms before returning to Louisiana. All of us wanted Saucony sneakers for school. My nanny brought me a pair. I thought I was all that and a bag of chips. She was always kind to me. She was always trying to expand my thinking and expose me to things and places outside of where we were raised. Of course, she had me reading while I was there. I knew about Harry Potter before the movies came out. We went to the library often. She would take us to eat out at different places. While she was at work, we would all go swim in the apartment complex pool. That took my mind off of everything back home until my cousin's best friend started being ugly to me. I told my cousin about it and she had a talk with her about mistreating me. Her best friend apologized, and she started treating me better. My cousin did not play behind me, and she still doesn't. I didn't know why her best friend didn't like me. I thought it was because she knew the guys who raped me. She grew up with them, so she probably felt like I should've kept my mouth closed like everyone else felt. Nevertheless, she changed her attitude towards me, and I didn't hold that against her.

I was anxious about starting middle school, but I was preparing myself. I wanted a fresh start. I wanted to show people that I wasn't this dumb daughter of a drug addict. I know you're probably thinking how I was getting prepared for middle school and I was only ten years old. Well, I started school when I was three years old and my birthday is in October. I made eleven years old while in the seventh grade.

When I got back from Houston, I didn't hear anything else about what happened to me. Life seemed normal again. Depression would come and go. I tried to smile, but I was dying on the inside. I hadn't seen my mom since she'd brought me home from the hospital. A few weeks after I got home, I finally saw her. She came to the house to rest and to get something to eat. When I got back, I met a boy. His name was Johnathon. He rode his bike to come see me all the time. I tried to meet him on the back street, away from our apartment so my grandmother wouldn't see us. One day, my mom saw us talking and walked up to us. She told him if he wanted to talk to me, he'd have to do it by my house. She told me not to ever let a man get comfortable not talking to me in front of my house. The trauma matured me in a way that it wasn't supposed to. I thought I was in love with him. He was gentle and kind. He would tell me how beautiful I was. He didn't care about any rumors he heard about me. He believed me when I told him that I would make up things to be cool. I told him about the abuse and molestation. He knew I had never been with anyone willingly. He wanted to fight the guys who'd touched me. I never saw anyone get that mad over me like he did. We would sneak and talk on the phone all the time. I was too young to talk on the phone with boys at the time. I would wait until my grandparents went to sleep to talk on the phone with him. He was a genius, but just like me, there were very few role models around him. He would achieve mastery on his standardized tests. He also played sports. He was in a grade higher than I was. He was always getting into trouble for fighting or having drugs in his possession. He became my best friend. One day, the neighbor who I was dry humping with, in the past, saw me standing in my back door. He came by the back door and tried to kiss me. Johnathon pulled up on his bike and saw him, but he also saw me pushing him away. He didn't say anything to me. He simply left on his bike and went home. When he got home, he called me. I told him what happened, that I was sorry and that I told him to stop and not to touch me. I pushed him away. The next day when we got out of school, Johnathon fought James. Of course, everyone blamed me. This was just one more thing to be mad at me about. I didn't tell him to fight him. I guess because of all the things I'd been through and all the things he knew about me, it angered him to see that. All the people in the neighborhood were mad at me. I couldn't win for losing. The only thing I was guilty of was dry humping with him and letting him tease me with people afterwards. I grew up with him, so regardless, I loved him, and I really didn't want them to fight. I just wished I could rewind time and fix that.

Johnathon was so mature for his age. I felt myself maturing gradually. I was actually starting to feel that light inside of me again. We would talk about going to college and our future plans. We talked about our goals and what we wanted in life. I was in the 7th grade and he was in the 8th grade. During the school year, we would wear each other's school IDs. Don't act like ya'll ain't never did that before. He would even let me wear his jacket. We would hug when we saw each other in the hallway. Thankfully, Johnathan and James made amends after the fight. Everything was going great. Johnathan and I came up with a not so good idea, one day. I don't know what made us come up with the brilliant idea of having him sneak into my house. I should've learned my lesson from the last time I tried to do that. My aunt tore me up, but I loved him so much and I thought that was the way to show someone you love them. It was my birthday. He said he wanted to come over and lay down with me, so I snuck him in. My anxiety was on ten the entire time. We laid in my bed, one thing led to another, and we attempted to have sex. It was very painful. He said that we would have to keep doing it, for it to feel better, but that never happened. He was still very nice to me. I thought that after we had sex, he would leave me alone, but he didn't. I would sneak him in all the time, but guess what happened? We fell asleep together one night and my grandfather woke up. He woke us up screaming and yelling. That woke my grandmother up from her sleep. She came running in the living room swinging her belt at me. My grandfather threw Johnathan out of the house with only his boxers on. My grandfather threw his clothes and shoes at him. It wasn't funny then, but I'm sure Johnathan was pissed. He loved those Converse tennis shoes. All I saw was those long shoes flying in the air and Johnathon took off running. My grandmother asked me what's wrong with me. I couldn't even respond. Here I go again, disappointing the people I loved. People in the neighborhood clowned me about it for weeks. They all saw it go down. I was punished for what felt like forever.

My grandfather used to take us to Breaux Bridge to his parents' house to play in their backyard. Whelp, I couldn't go there anymore. I was punished. I couldn't go play outside. I had to do extra chores. I couldn't talk on the phone anymore. I had to go to sleep early. My little sister asked me why did I do that? I couldn't answer her. I imagined that I wasn't being a good example for her at all. She couldn't have understood that I was only looking for love. Looking for love in anything that would show me kindness. I didn't know that love and kindness were not the same thing. You can be nice to people and not love them. I didn't understand that principle. I was too young to understand that. No one taught me the true meaning.

That next day, I got to school, and I had to tell my friends what happened. Kate and Mya couldn't believe I got caught or that I was really having sex. I would see Johnathon at school, but he barely said anything to me. I knew something was wrong. He would hug me when he saw me in the hallway. He was still dry and distant with me.

Chapter 8

The Bible says, in 1 Corinthians 4:8, "Love is patient, love is kind. It does not envy, it does not boast, it is not proud. It does not dishonor others, it is not self-seeking, it is not easily angered, it keeps no record of wrongs. Love does not delight in evil but rejoices with the truth. It always protects, always trusts, always hopes, always perseveres. Love never fails. I never understood that. That's why I so easily took whatever was given to me. I'm turning the combination on my padlock again. At eleven years old, I experienced my first heartbreak. My heart had been broken by irresponsible adults. My heart had been broken by drug dealers who could care less about their lives or anyone else's life. I had been failed and abandoned, and all those things happened against my will. This time, I actually thought someone loved me. This time, I willingly gave my heart away. I truly believed that I was going to spend the rest of my life with him. I believed that he cared for me. I poured out all my secrets and dreams to him. When I was finally able to talk to him on the phone, he told me that we had to break up. He told me he had a new girlfriend and he was able to go to her house without a problem. Her parents were more accepting of their relationship. Everything came crashing down on me at once. My understanding of love came from a hurt place. I went to a place that caused more pain on myself. That heartbreak put me in a place where I no longer cared who I gave myself to. I began a long journey of promiscuity. A piece of me would leave every time they would get up and leave. I was just passing out permission slips for people to penetrate my mind, my body and my soul. All they had to do was be nice to me and they could have whatever it was they wanted from me. I was destroying my reputation even more than what it was. I was bleeding on myself and on others. My grandparents were constantly catching me in the act; sneaking boy after boy inside of our apartment. I was letting men twice my age take advantage of me and my brokenness repeatedly. I built up a wall, and I told myself that I didn't care about it all. I thought that if I acted as if I was a boy, I wouldn't get my feelings hurt. I thought that if I just asked for sex, it would save me the trouble of being lied to and manipulated, all for one purpose. Somehow, I found that liberating at the time. I felt like I had control of my own body and I could do whatever I wanted to do with it. The downside of it was being called a hoe and worsening an already tarnished reputation. The great plan I had for middle school went down the drain. I was always in the principal's office for trying to be the class clown. Here I am with a new set of teachers that didn't take me seriously. They didn't care if I was being treated unkindly by the other students because of my behavior. My friend Mya had a few classes with me, but her other classes were honors classes.

I would get teased about my hair. My teachers would make fun of me, also. My grandmother didn't really know how to do my hair like the other children. All she could do was try to put my hair in a ponytail. One day, my rubber band popped, and my hair was all over my head after P.E. My science teacher made so many jokes about my hair; saying that it looked like a tornado blew through it. My friend Mya asked if we could be excused to the restroom. She had a small brush and a rubber band. She put some water in her hands to put in my hair and brushed it back in place. She put some up and some down to make it look like something. I think it was because I seemed so strong, people didn't have a problem with being hurtful. I appreciated every single time someone decided to be nice to me. Between being bullied by students and teachers and missing my mom, suicidal thoughts started raiding my mind. I thought that maybe if I wasn't here, people would learn to appreciate me. I didn't have the guts to really go through with it, but it crossed my mind. Why should I be here? I'm literally a door mat. I was something people could just use to wipe their feet on.

My behavior was getting worse. I was so angry. One day, I was coming from P.E. and a group of girls who were pretty popular called me over. One of them took douches out of her book sack. If you don't know what a douche is, it's what women use to cleanse their private part. They put one in my hand and squirted the other one on my shirt. I ran into the library. My shirt was wet. I told the librarian what happened. She gave me some paper towels to clean up with. She told me to go straight to the principal's office to tell her what happened. I didn't go though. I left out of the library and went sit in the bathroom for a while and cried. I tried to talk myself into going tell the principal, but I didn't want to be considered a snitch, if I did. After much contemplating, I went anyway. I knew I should've followed my first mind. When I went to tell the principal, she asked me their names and she took me with her to confront them. She didn't really tell them anything. She asked me why I thought they wanted to give me that. I shrugged my shoulders, but I knew she was insinuating that they had every right to give me that, because I smelled. She allowed them to go back to class and she asked me if I wanted to call someone to pick me up or bring me a change of clothes. I told her no, only because I knew no one would be able to pick me up. I really did want to go home though. As she walked me to class, she told me that she had been getting complaints about my body odor. I wanted to tell her what was going on with me, but the way she humiliated me in front of the girls, I knew I couldn't trust her to truly care about my depression. I told her I would work on it. She asked me if I was bathing at home and I said, "Yes". The kids at school would tease me about the odor and about my mom's drug addiction. They teased me about my shoes. They teased me about my hair. Seemingly, everything was completely wrong with my existence. It wasn't just the girls. The guys would tease me, also. I tried to be down with the people who were bullying me, so I began bullying people, also. The teachers were partaking in the bullying, as well.

I hated going to social studies class. I was convinced my teacher was a racist. We had a hurricane and she complained about black people having 3 baskets full of groceries because they had gotten emergency food stamps. She said she had to wait in line for hours to check out. She had a lot to say about our hair textures and hairstyles too. I find it to be very insane to put yourself in a career where you must be of service to people that you don't like. Well, one day, she stood up and said it smelled musty in the class, and she was going to put some deodorant on the desk. Whoever was musty needed to grab it and put some on. As she was saying it, she was looking me directly in my face. The whole class busted out laughing, except for the mature students or the ones who didn't find it funny. She laughed and told me, "Just get the deodorant and go to the bathroom. You are killing us in here". I put my head down and stared at my desk. I tried to be strong in that moment and not let her see that she was getting to me. If my behavior was an issue before, it became so much worse after this.

I would always get a probation card or be in the adjustment center in high school. I took my grandmother's lighter from home and brought it to school. One of the dumbest decisions I've ever made. It was just months after

9/11. I decided to burn some paper in class and throw it in the trash can. They called the police on me and everything. I got expelled for the remainder of the school year and was sent to a place where misbehaved students would go, called "The Base". I met some interesting people from different schools there. We had a lot of fun, even though it was a school for misbehaved kids. There were security guards and policemen there. They seemed to care about us. They were strict, but they always wanted the best for us. If you were well behaved, they would send you back to school after a few months. You determined how long you were going to be there. I stayed there for the remainder of the school year. I was trying to show off and be hard while I was over there.

I was fighting and being disrespectful, being promiscuous and sneaking guys in the house over and over again. That never satisfied me. I was trying to fill a void that I didn't realize I was trying to fill. It seemed like every time I had sex with someone, a piece of me would be stolen. I kept that cycle going. I was finally able to go back to school, and I tried to push my way through. I was still fighting and being disrespectful to teachers and my peers. They sent me back to "The Base". My grandmother was so disappointed in me. No one ever stopped to ask me why I was behaving that way. No one asked me if I was ok. I was just supposed to take and take and take, and I started to become the very things I hated. I had to remain at "The Base" until it was time for me to go to high school. I had a teacher at "The Base", named Mr. Walters. He had talks with me about boys and how I should carry myself better. He would tell me that it was more to life than boys. He told me that I was still so young, and I had time to figure it out. I hadn't even told him what I was going through. He set the tone for my next level. He told me I was beautiful and that if someone truly loved me, they would wait until we were old enough to get married and start a family. He said that I was a beautiful young lady and guys were only after one thing. He said you'll find someone that will love you for your heart and not what you can give them. He took his time with all of us. I later found out my first-grade teacher was his stepmom. I'm referring to the teacher who would put holy oil on our foreheads and play gospel music in the classroom. I felt a light growing on the inside of me again. At that moment, I thought maybe it was returning. I heard this quote "What you feed will grow and what you starve will die". I was starving my depression and abandonment, but I had no food to feed my light. I loved the way I was starting to feel, but all the negativity I was surrounded by was throwing dirt on my light. In Genesis chapter 26, it tells us a story about Isaac. Isaac had wells that were making him prosperous. Because of jealousy, he was forced to leave his wells and go dig up new ones, but everywhere he went the Philistines would throw dirt on it. Every time he moved on and tried to dig up another well, they would still throw dirt on what he was trying to create. They wanted to start conflict with him. Finally, after traveling a little further, he came to a place called Rehoboth. Rehoboth means "open space". It seemed like everywhere he went, they tried to close him in with contention and strife. So, God made room for him. He became seven times more prosperous than he already was. He persisted, even when they repeatedly threw dirt on his wells. He didn't give up. He didn't throw in the towel, but I didn't have faith like that just yet. I had a moment of happiness that I thought was something beautiful. That teacher watered some seeds that were inside of me without even knowing it.

I made a promise to myself that I wasn't going to be promiscuous anymore. I wasn't, but I still struggled with my self-worth because here I was, only thirteen years old with a bad reputation. My reputation was longer than my hair, my age and my height. The more I tried to rise up, the more I would get pushed back down. I didn't know how to be strong and courageous. So, I just took whatever the world decided to give me. Whatever they wanted to label me as, I was just fine with being that. I took on this "free-spirited" persona. My comical skills never left. It was my coping mechanism. No one can say that they've ever seen me break down. I always kept myself entertained. My bedroom was closed for business though. I wasn't participating in that anymore. Of course, when I said no to sex, I got treated badly and even called out of my name. I didn't care though, because I was not going to let anyone see me sweat. I prepared myself to head into high school with a fresh start. I've always been a planner. I just couldn't get the "doing" part right.

My aunt was in and out, meaning sometimes she lived with us and sometimes she didn't. My cousin, Shyann, from Alabama, also came to live with us. I treated her badly, only because my grandmother started giving her so much attention. We got along for the most part. I just didn't want to share my grandmother with anyone. I could see why my grandmother loved her so much. It was because she was sweet and soft spoken. I don't think I ever heard her fuss before. I was already trying to fight through being "jacked up". She couldn't have possibly known that. She was always so timid and soft. She would just brush me off. We were on again and off again best friends. One night, I put her and my friend Brittany on the dating hotline. My name on the hotline was "Red". On the dating hotline, you could talk on the phone with guys from other cities. We thought that was the funniest and coolest thing in the world. Well, I did. I guess because I could pretend to be someone I wasn't. I could be this great person and they loved my voice. I have this Cajun accent that almost sounds like I'm from the islands. It's a down south Louisiana thing. So, my life at this point consisted of me making me smile. I wanted to do anything that would make me laugh and have a good time. I became the life of the party. I was finally reclaiming my life and being a fun, outspoken, spunky girl. I was just masking my issues.

My grandparents were planning on moving. I know I probably should've been overjoyed about this decision, but I wasn't. We moved from the projects into a beautiful pink house. It pained me to leave my friends. My friend Phaedra was a mother now. Kirsten went away for a while for some trouble she got into, but before she left, she told me to be a better person. She told me I wasn't like everyone else and that fighting and getting into trouble wasn't a good look. She was always my big sister and protector. All I had to do was tell her that someone was picking on me and she was coming. She would make me fight too. She would tell me if you don't hit her, I'm gon' beat you! I was scared of her too. I would fight 2 and 3 girls at a time just so I wouldn't get beat up by Kirsten. She just loved me that much. She wanted me to be able to defend myself against bullies.

One day, Shyann and I were hanging outside. She said it sounded like someone was screaming our names from the house. We stood by the door and heard someone yelling again. It was my aunt calling us in the house. She was sitting on the toilet in the bathroom when we finally went inside. I thought she wanted us to hand her some toilet tissue, but that's not what she wanted at all. She had a mirror with some white powder on it. She told us to come sniff it. We both paused for a second, but because we feared her, we sniffed the lines. She told us to open our mouth and she rubbed it on our gums, also. Then, she told us to go back and play outside. We ran outside and instantly we were high. We couldn't stop laughing and seemed like the trees were twirling around us. We were making snow angels in the grass. We were high as a kite. After we came down off the high, we talked about it and we were so mad that we did it. We talked about the impact drugs and alcohol has had on our family. It was a horrible experience. We made a promise that we would never do it again, even if she tried to force us to do it. We pinky promised and never did it again. Neither of us ever wanted to try it again. A few days passed and I found myself laying in my bed thinking about it and getting angry. Why would she do that to us? What if we would've gotten hooked on it and been walking around like Pookie from the movie "New Jack City".

Chapter 9

My grandmother worked hard to take care of us. My grandfather got injured offshore and received a big settlement. That's how we purchased the house and our brand new, black Yukon Denali. They were so busy trying to keep everything together. They couldn't have known what was going on in every minute of every hour. They tried their best. I always felt like my aunt had an issue with my grandmother taking care of me and my sister. She was my grandparents' last child. I think she felt like we imposed on their relationship, but we really didn't. She was still very spoiled by them.

My cousin and I never spoke of that day again. We just pretended it never happened. At this house, we didn't have a tree in the yard, but our neighbors did. One day, I went sit under the tree and the strangest thing happened. A leaf fell on my shoulder. As I've done in the past, I ripped it to pieces and watched the wind take it away.

I had a guy friend named Bradley who would come spend time with me every day after school. I talked to him about all my issues. My grandparents were ok with me talking outside, but I wasn't allowed to bring guys into their house. We were able to talk on the phone, also. One day, my aunt saw us sitting on the porch and she threatened him and told him to leave. I told her I was going to tell my grandmother on her. She said that she would tell my grandmother that I was kissing him. I begged her not to do that because it wasn't true. She said she wouldn't tell my grandmother, if I agreed to have sex with her well-known gangster friend. I was just getting in good graces with my grandparents, so I did it against my better judgement. I was 13 years old. He had to be well in his early 40's. I grew up around him. He was a close friend of the family. She said all he wanted to do was have oral sex with me. She told me to make sure I shaved. At that time, I thought having pubic hair was cool. She told me to shave because he was going to perform oral sex on me. I was literally scared out of my mind. I'd only had sex with one person willingly. I shaved, got dressed and left in the car with her. During the ride there, she explained the terms of the arrangement. I could see her lips moving, but my mind was in another place. I couldn't believe I was about to do this. She blackmailed me. Later, I found out I wasn't the only girl she would get to have sex with him. He was paying her for it. The whole transaction was disgusting. He was overweight and old. He smelled like chicken and Kool-Aid. He was rubbing and touching on me. After he finished, we left. My aunt handed me $30. She reminded me of Ronnie from the movie "The Players Club". The only difference was that, I couldn't beat her up like

Diamond beat Ronnie at the end of the movie. She would've knocked me out. It seemed like every time I would try to get up and do the right thing, something would pull me back down. I stopped talking to my friend Bradley afterwards. I felt out of touch with myself. I felt dirty. I went down the same road I promised myself I wouldn't go down again. I started letting people take advantage of me, being promiscuous and not caring about myself again. My mom was still doing her thing and my dad treated me as if I didn't exist. When was I ever going to get a break? I thought because I held things together so well that made me strong; that made me superwoman. I thought if they didn't see me cry, I was unstoppable, but on the inside, I was screaming for help. There is no place scarier than the darkness that lies on the inside of you. It makes you bitter and angry. I was heading for destruction in the worst way. The friends that I was gravitating toward didn't make it any better. If they were able to get a laugh at my expense, nothing else mattered. People don't really understand the pain of constantly having things stolen from you when you never intended to give it away; when you never asked for it to be taken, but it gets taken anyway. My bad behavior was a cry for help, even though I thought I was protecting myself.

When I got to high school, I was still being my silly, obnoxious self. I was doing my best to terrorize the teachers and the students. My favorite thing to do was to play pranks on people. The best part about being there was that after two long years, I was finally reunited with Shelly and Cliff.

We've been rolling since pre-k. They loved me-flaws and all. Of course, Mya, Kate, Kerri and Bianca were there also. Yasmin and Kylon were forced to go to the other high school, because of their addresses. The craziest thing about my behavior is that the people I grew up with never encouraged it. They saw the gold that I couldn't see in myself. I tried to attach myself to the new people that I'd met along the way. Unfortunately, they only wanted me around because I made them laugh, and I was fun to be around.

I met some great people in high school though. Tianna and Leslie were the cutest, skinny light skinned girls I'd ever met. They both had long hair. I met Kristy, Nina and Porcha in high school also. These 3 girls were best friends and they used to dress alike all the time. That was their signature style. I was closer to Kristy in their group, but they were all sweet. Deon became my friend in high school also. He was mixed, had long braids and gold teeth in his mouth. He was the coolest guy you could ever meet. He would give me the shirt off his back if he had to. Then, there was Karli and Ashton. They were my girls. Karli's mom didn't really want her hanging with me and looking back, I can see why. Contrary to popular belief, I have never been an influencer of things that I was partaking in. I always did my own thing, and it didn't matter to me if my friends were different. I've always had a love for people of all walks of life. I think we focus so much on wanting people to be more like us that we don't get to enjoy individuality. Ashton was a cheerleader and her mom was a principal at an elementary school right next door to our school. Surprisingly, her mom was cool with us being friends. I was going through a lot that they didn't know about and things I couldn't possibly tell them. I had to keep up the persona of being this strong, crazy, wild child. All my friends had different personalities and I loved all of them for it.

After ruining my freshman year in high school, I decided to try out for the dance team with my friend Shelly. We practiced really hard. I made it, but she didn't. I never understood how I made it and she didn't. I messed up on the routine and they still selected me. I later heard that the older members on the team cried because I was selected. Although my heart broke because Shelly didn't make the team, I knew this was what I needed at that time. My friend really wanted to be on the team. My mom was so happy for me. My grandmother eagerly paid for everything. I thought I would be embarrassed that my mom showed up to events and parades to take pictures of me, but I wasn't. She would take pictures of me and scream my name really loud. Surprisingly, my dad came to see me dance too. Everything was good. The dance team sponsor, Mrs. Janson, did not play with us. She expected us to present ourselves in a lady-like manner, at all times. She knew my background and that my grades were not up to par, but she always assured me that she believed in me to do better. She wanted me to excel. She saw something in me that very few people did. Mrs. Janson really made a big impact on my life.

The girls on the dance team tried their best to love on me, even though they would tease me behind my back about the odor problem. With joining the team, I'd created a problem for myself because now I had to keep switching deodorants because nothing would work. I was taken to the doctor for it. The doctor said that I had overactive sweat glands. Honestly, I thought it was the result of me mistreating my body when I went through depression. We all had a heart to heart one day, and I shared some things with them. I didn't want them to be uncomfortable around me and I didn't want to be uncomfortable around them. The conversation stemmed from one of my teammates having issues at home with her mom. She was crying and saying that she hated her mom. She was a privileged girl. Her family had money and gave her the best of everything. I used that moment to give her my testimony about my relationship with my mom and why I was the way that I was. I expressed to her why I still loved my mom, despite what I'd gone through with her. There was not one dry eye in the circle. In that moment, I felt our sisterhood grow stronger. This little troubled girl from the projects was doing toe touches, back bends, leaps, kicks, turns and pointing her toes.

The best part was dancing with the band. Tianna, Angel, Kylie and I were on the back row. The band would brag about us. We did our thing! We thought we were dancing dolls. My favorite song that the band played was "Cold Hearted Snake". We danced our butts off in parades and in the stands for football games. I found my spark again. It was great! Of course, I was still a comedian. I couldn't help myself, but for the most part, my behavior did a 360. I hadn't seen my mom in a few months and that was the only thing that was bothering me at that point.

Being a jokester has its pros and cons. I was such a comedian that anything I said made my friends laugh and laugh uncontrollably. I was just that funny. The people I grew up with knew me more in depth, but my school friends automatically assumed that my grandmother and grandfather were my parents. One night, my friends and I were coming from the state fair. On our way home, we saw a lady walking barefoot and she looked like she had been in a fight. You could imagine that they died of laughter when I began to scream, "Stop the car. That's my mom". When the tears began to fall from my eyes, they realized that it was not a joke. The driver stopped the car. I begged her to get in the car. Her clothes were dirty, and her eyes were swollen. She said, "I'll meet you later. I promise. I have something I need to do". My friends began to

console me. I could tell they were in shock because everyone was silent all the way to my house. I waited for her. I sat on my porch and waited, but she never showed up. I sat there and reflected on our walks and talks. She would always encourage me and tell me I was her best friend. I feared for her life out there. I feared that someone would hurt her. For the first time in a long time, I broke down that night. I cried until it hurt. I just wanted my mom to be healthy.

Shortly after that, she was arrested, and this time my grandparents couldn't get her out. She had to go to St. Gabriel woman's prison in St. Gabriel, La. That's the big prison. It wasn't like our parish jail. That's where women went who had to do hard time. We used to go visit my mom at the parish jail, but this place was further away, so we only went to see her twice. They sentenced her to 10 years in prison. I was heartbroken and happy at the same time. That night I broke down again. I asked God to save her. I asked Him to take her off the streets. If this was his way of doing it, I was fine with it. The other part of me was sad because of how much I would miss her. She was my best friend and my mother. Drugs took her from us and now this. In our town, there's a big celebration called "The Sugarcane Festival". I remember getting a shirt made with her picture on it. I wore it for the festival. It said, "Free Rosh". Rosh was one of her nicknames. She would write us letters and call us whenever she could. My grandmother was constantly sending things to her to make sure she was comfortable. Wait! How could I forget? During the course of all this, my mom had 2 more children. Yes, I now had 2 more siblings. I now had 2 little brothers. They were named Semaj and Jeremiah. They were little babies when my mom left for prison. My Aunt Marie took my little brother Semaj. She lost a son when I was a baby. Due to mistaken identity, the cops killed him when he was only 16 years old. Semaj brought a lot of joy to her life. Not that he could ever replace her son, but he filled a void that she had because of losing her son. We got to see Semaj a lot because my aunt and grandmother were very close. She took such good care of him. My other brother, Jeremiah, was supposed to live with another aunt, but by the time we got to the hospital, she had signed him over to another lady that we didn't know. She didn't keep him from us, but everyone was on edge about it because we didn't know her. Now I'm the oldest of 3 girls and 2 boys. I knew I had to get myself together and I had to get myself together quickly.

My friend Karli kept my mind off of my troubles. We had so much fun together. We would go shopping. She would do my hair. I would spend the night at her house. She became a big sister to me. We met as members of the dance team. She had me taking care of my hair and skin, and we got our nails done together. We partied together. I was finally being a normal girl, but my reputation wouldn't let me live it down. It followed me everywhere I went. I was always grateful for my friends because being connected to me wasn't a good look for their reputation, but they loved me anyway.

I had to put my personal life aside after we found out my grandmother had stage IV lung cancer. The devastation that brought to my family was unreal. My grandmother was the backbone of the family and not just for me and my siblings, but for all of us. My cousin Shyann was living with us at the time. Just to show how much of a big heart my grandmother had, imagine this. My grandfather had an outside child. He had a daughter with another woman. His daughter was my age and her mom passed away. So, she had to come live with us too. My grandmother didn't treat her any different from the way she treated us. She had a talk with us to let us know why she was coming to live with us. She made it clear that we were to treat her nicely because her mom had passed away. We were teenage girls, so of course, we bumped heads, fussed and fought with each other. Then, we'd love on each other later. It was a never-ending cycle, but my grandmother took care of all of us. Her sisters and her brother adored her. They always came to visit her from New Orleans. She was loved and honored by so many that the news of cancer was devastating for everyone. I guess I can say that holding things in and pretending to be ok was a trait that I inherited from her. I never saw her cry, even when my grandfather cheated. I never saw her cry for my mom or her other children. She started her chemo treatments, and she began to lose weight right away. Her hair started to fall out. That was such a tough pill for me to swallow. I was stressing out and still trying to keep it together. I couldn't go with her to chemo because she went during school hours. That was hard for me.

My godmother had just beat breast cancer a few years prior to my grandmother being diagnosed. I was trying to stay positive about it and think about how my godmother fought and beat her cancer. My grandmother was much older and weaker than my godmother though. My mind was all over the place. She continued with her treatments and she continued working. Her coworkers knew her situation, and they helped her tremendously. We were even in a magazine, a local magazine called "Lifestyle". They did an article on my grandmother's life. They mentioned how she was taking care of us while fighting cancer and having an incarcerated daughter.

Summer

This is the hottest season of them all.
The sun shines so bright that it shines on our flaws and our glory. Not only can you see your shadow following you, but you can also see goodness and mercy following you too. It's okay to look for shade. Just make sure it's the right tree.

Chapter 10

Isaiah 43:2 says, "When you pass through the waters, I will be with you; and through the rivers, they shall not overwhelm you; when you walk through fire you shall not be burned, and the flame shall not consume you." No matter how hot it was for me, the fire never consumed me. No matter how much I felt like I had water up to my neck, I didn't drown. While dealing with past trauma and my grandmother fighting for her life, I knew something had to give. My boyfriend, at the time, was constantly lying to me. He made me feel less than I was. I was so done with feeling less than. I was over being the class clown. I felt like I was about to explode into a million pieces. My friend and dance team member's parents are pastors. She was always talking about God. She could never go to parties with us, and she was expected to present herself a certain way. We teased her about that often. One day, she was on my heart all day, for some reason. I felt like I needed to talk to her. I needed her to pray for me. I waited until school was over to talk to her. We had practice that day. I knew that would be the perfect time to speak with her. I walked over to her and said,

"Angel, can I talk to you in private?" She said sure in her little sweet voice. She had a porcelain doll face with rosy cheeks and a big smile. She was more than happy to talk to me. We sat on a bench while the other girls were warming up for practice. I began telling her about my grandmother's cancer diagnosis, how much I missed my mom and how I felt so alone. I told her that I was ready for a change in my life and that I was tired of these never-ending cycles. I was tired of being hurt, then acting out of my emotions, which led me to do more things to hurt myself. I asked her to do something with me that I'd never asked anyone to do before. I asked her to pray with me. Her sweet voice got bolder and deeper as she began to pray for me. She grabbed my hands and went in. It felt like she called heaven down in our practice area. After she finished praying for me, she said I'll always be here to pray for you whenever you need. We were only 16 years old. At that moment, I made a promise to myself that if I ever had children that I would raise them to be just like her. I'd want my children to be of service to anyone in need. She wasn't judgmental at all. I never saw her laugh at anyone's pain or say anything harmful toward anyone. She changed my life that day. The feeling I felt from praying is a feeling I wanted all the time. I felt God's love in that moment. Things didn't magically get better for me, but I got better. It didn't matter what came my way, I handled all my problems with grace. I began praying every day and every night. That didn't stop things from happening to me. I just believed that I could get up from whatever situation I was in.

The dance team did a lot for me. Our sponsor Mrs. Janson was always rooting for me. The first year I made the team, our captain Delilah became my big sister. She mentored me until she left for college. She took me everywhere she went. She showed me how to be elegant and graceful. I went with her to her debutante practices. She was a debutante for Alpha Kappa Alpha Sorority, Incorporated. She had big dreams and aspirations to be a dancing doll for Southern University. Being around young women who had standards and morals altered my way of thinking. I was truly evolving. I couldn't leave my personality out though. Of course, I kept my sense of humor. It wasn't going anywhere. Some people liked it, some people didn't. Either way, I couldn't help it.

The guidance counselor at school, Mrs. Hart, checked out my grades and sent me a letter. She was a member of Delta Sigma Theta Sorority, Incorporated, and they hosted a debutante ball and a host of events that went along with it. When I received the letter to be a part of something so significant, I was shocked. A debutante is an upper-class young lady making her first appearance in a fashionable society. I was a tea girl my junior year in high school. I began my journey to do the same thing Delilah did, but with a different sorority. I was preparing to become a debutante. With being bullied and teased, getting into fights and disrupting class, my first two years of high school did not go as planned. The next two years turned around in my favor. People who used to look at me with disgust were actually speaking to me and wanting me to be around. I was named the most comical girl my junior and senior year of high school. I was getting ready to make my debut to the world, and everything was flowing so well for me. My grandmother was so proud. She bragged on me all the time. Her cancer didn't stop her from pushing herself harder. She was helping me get prepared for my debut also. I'm happy I was able to experience it. I made some everlasting bonds with girls from different places around Louisiana.

One night, we had girl's night at a hotel. We were asked what kind of guys we liked. We all lied and said that we liked nerds and guys who make good grades. One of the debs, Kyla, was in a wheelchair. She was born that way, but that didn't stop her from achieving anything she set her mind to. She made good grades and had a bright future ahead of her. We all gave each other nicknames. My nick name was "Retarto" because of my sense of humor. I gave Kyla the nickname "Zoom". It was inspired by the song "Zoom" that Lil' Boosie came out with a year or so before we started practicing. It was Kyla's turn to answer what kind of guys she liked. Guess what she said? She said she likes thugs. I could not stop laughing. I didn't expect that to come from her, but at least she wasn't faking it like we all were. They told us to choose someone to sleep next to. I called myself choosing Kyla because I really didn't like sleeping with people. When I tell you, she kicked me in my back all night. I woke up the next morning scared as hell. I told everyone, "Ya'll, Kyla can walk". They laughed at me and said I was tripping. I really believed she could until I learned about nerves and that they still work in that type of condition. I can't believe I thought that. She would laugh at me and encourage my silliness. We had such a good experience.

My grandfather came to practice with me because we had to practice the father daughter dance. My father was still inactive in my life. My grandfather filled in, in every area. I had never seen my grandfather dance ever in life. During practice he always stepped on my toes, but I just smiled and pretended that he was doing a great job. He was so happy to get fitted for his tuxedo. He even took me to get my dress made. My grandmother was so happy to attend the mother daughter tea with me. I was finally making everyone around me proud. My friend Charles partnered with me for the debutante ball. He didn't miss a practice. I wasn't dating anyone at the time, nor did I have any male friends that I liked. I was serious about changing. It was confirmed that things were turning around for me when a childhood friend of mine saw me sitting outside. He stopped his car to talk to me. I hadn't seen him in a while, except for seeing him on MySpace. My friend Cliff had my MySpace layout lit.

It would light up, and it had my name in the background. Cliff also decided to document our entire senior year. He called it "Da Berry". We had some great times. We phone pranked people during our senior skip days. Can you believe that I was in charge of coordinating our senior skip days? We would all meet up at Jaden's house. He had a huge house with a big pool in the back yard. Now that I think about it, he kind of looked like Barack Obama back then. Well let me finish telling you about my childhood friend that popped up on me. His name is Landon. He had long hair, and he wore it braided. I knew how to braid hair, so he started coming over to get his hair braided. I had a huge crush on him. He was so goofy and fun. We clowned about everything, and he was gentle and kind. He was about 2 years older than I was, so he was out of school and working. My grandmother liked him, and she didn't like any of the guys I dated in the past. She didn't allow me to have anybody inside to watch TV with me, but she would let him, and she even treated us to dinner sometimes. He came to see me every day when he got off of work. I was completely enjoying my senior year. The only bad part about it was that my grandmother's health was declining. She was losing so much weight. One day, she was trying to do laundry and fell in the laundry room. She had a big knot on her forehead. I fussed at her like I was her mom. I'd told her to stop doing so much and to let me take care of everything. I told her I didn't want her doing anything that could possibly cause her harm.

Our pictures came in from the mother daughter tea that we attended when I made my debut. I stared at those pictures and cried. I couldn't imagine life without her. I needed her to beat this stupid cancer. When I was a little girl, she was a chain smoker. She would light the next cigarette with the cigarette she was currently smoking. She even smoked while she combed my hair. She would drop ashes in my hair and pop me if I jumped or pouted about it. My grandfather told her she had to stop smoking because she couldn't smoke in our new house. I always felt like she stopped smoking and brought this house for us. If it was up to her, she would've been comfortable living in the projects. She wanted so much more for us than that environment had to offer. The only thing that was stressing me out at this point was her illness. I put aside my feelings about my mom being locked away, and I focused on making my grandmother proud until she did something I never thought she'd do. I was in my room listening to music. I was jamming to John Legend and Keyshia Cole. She made a big pot of okra with shrimps and sausage in it. She cooked smothered pork chops on the side. I heard her yell my name. When I jumped out of my bed and made it to the living room, my mom's ex-husband was there, sitting on the sofa. She asked me to make him a plate of food to go. I paused for the longest time because I hadn't seen him since I was 10 years old. At that point, I was 16 years old. He looked at me with this crazy grin. I walked out and went to fix his plate. I can't believe I fixed the plate. I fixed it, handed it to him and went to my room. I was so angry. I thought about all the things I should've done. I should've slapped him or threw the food at his face. I was trying to forget his face. What was he doing here? Why would she call me to make his plate? I know she was feeling bad, but he could've gone to get a burger from somewhere else. He didn't need a plate of food from us. After he left, I went to her room and asked her why he was there. She said it was because she's getting sick, and she needed to talk to him about helping financially with my little sister. She said she had to get my mom to sign something from jail to get my dad to pay child support, as well. She hugged me and said she was sorry for making me uncomfortable. My anger dissipated as I looked at her fragile body. Her head was bald and shiny from the chemo. I understood what she was doing. She needed help, but her need for help opened a door for him to penetrate me. Not physically, but mentally.

A few days after he visited, he called to speak with my sister. I didn't see a name on the caller ID box, so I answered it. When I answered it, he asked me who I was. I said my name. I didn't recognize his voice immediately, so I asked him who he wanted to speak to. He said, "I see you're all grown up now and looking good". I paused for a moment. I knew exactly who was on the other end of the phone. I told him never to address me again. Don't look at me. Don't speak to me, and I told him that I should've thrown that plate of food in his face. He laughed at me, as if my threats meant nothing to him. I told him how disgusting he was and that I hoped he rotted in hell. He asked if he could buy me a gift. He told me that he's messed with so many other girls, but they didn't give him the feeling I did. I hung up the phone. He kept calling. I went in my sister's room, threw the phone on her bed and told her that her dad was calling to talk to her. I ran to the bathroom to vomit. I literally got nauseous at the thought of him doing what he did to me to another little innocent girl. I thought about him holding her down, putting tape on her mouth, tying her hands behind her back, making her watch porn, beating her if she didn't do what he said, and touching her in places she didn't ask to be touched. I felt so sick for the rest of the day. Why was he so evil? I told Landon about it and it angered him. He was just as disgusted as I was. He told me to let him know if he ever called again, but he never did, at least not while I was around.

My grandmother bought me a cell phone. My minutes weren't free until after 9:00 PM though. I hated to get text messages before 9:00 because that was using my minutes. I didn't like using the house phone because my grandpa would always eavesdrop on our conversations. My grandparents really liked Landon. They would allow him to take me out to eat and to the movies. I had never been on a real date before. That took my mind off so much that was happening around me. I still couldn't believe that man had the audacity to talk to me like that. My anger for him was building up all over again. I tried to forget about him and everything he'd put me through, but that phone call put me in another space. I dreamt about killing him. I came up with elaborate plans to shoot and even stab him. I wanted to tie his hands up, put tape on his mouth and cut off his manhood; the same way he took so much from me without my permission. I wanted him to suffer. I had thoughts of chopping his body up and throwing it in Bayou Teche. This only forced me to start writing poetry again to clear my mind. There were a lot of things about me that I didn't disclose to my friends or the people around me. I just wanted them to see me as an easy, breezy, funny, cool girl.

Right after that, I was kicked off the dance team because my grades weren't up to par and we had a new sponsor. I was so upset. I felt personally attacked because I knew I wasn't her cup of tea. I was loud and spunky. She gravitated toward the more reserved girls. The reserved girls didn't like her though. I cried for about 2 days. The dance team was my life, and I was on track to receive my letterman jacket. They didn't put me on probation or give me a warning. I was just kicked off. I still danced on the sideline at the pep rallies though. My back-row crew was upset also. They couldn't believe I got kicked off. I shook it off, and I forgave the new sponsor. She was only doing her job. Sometimes, we take things personally that are not meant to be taken personally. Everybody is not always out to get us. Everything I'd been through thus far, made it seem that way sometimes. I had this overwhelming feeling that everyone was against me and no one wanted me to have anything or be anything.

Later that year, I was crowned queen of the winter formal. It was the first time our school had ever had a winter formal event. Everyone voted for me. I was so shocked when my name was announced, and I was given the crown.

I couldn't believe it. My grandmother was so proud of me. She kept my tiara in her glass case where she kept all her nice angels and crystals. I had a minor setback for a major come back. I'd come too far to turn back now. I couldn't let what I went through with my stepdad or getting kicked off the dance team detour me from my mission to graduate and go to college. I just wanted to be a better person all around. My teachers helped me pull through by giving me extra credit assignments. I failed the math portion of the leap test, so I had to take it over the summer. I passed it, and I received an extra credit for going to summer school. I made it by the skin of my teeth, Ya'll.

Homecoming was near. My boyfriend was my date to the dance. Everyone looked surprised to see him with me. I had a proud look on my face like, "Yassss, you see me, Boo. What ya'll thought?". We laughed and clowned the entire night. My grandmother made sure she bought my outfit from a boutique. We danced and took pictures at the dance. He started being there for me through everything. He told me he was ready to take me to prom, but my grandmother's finances weren't where she would've liked it to be because of her health. It was kind of depressing because it was my senior year, and I really wanted to go to prom. My friend Ashton assured me that everything would work out for me. Next thing I knew, Anna and I were on our way to Houston. We went spend the weekend with my nanny. I told her about my grandmother's hardships and how I probably wasn't going to prom because we couldn't afford it. I tried to stay positive about it. When we got to Houston, I had no idea that her and my nanny had already planned to hook me up. We went to so many stores. We tried every department store in the mall, but nothing was working out. We went to a dress store. There were wedding gowns and prom dresses. It was nice, elegant stuff. It was all so pricey, but my godmother made me try on dresses anyway. I fell in love with this champagne colored dress with peach sequin designs on the breast area. That dress was almost $400, so I took it off. Anna and I went back to the car. Then, here comes my godmother walking out of the store with a big, long bag. She said, "I love you dearly", and handed me this expensive, Alfred Angelo gown. Once I unzipped the bag, I realized it was the dress I'd fallen in love with. In that very moment, I felt like Cinderella. Not that my grandmother was the wicked stepmother or anything. It was just that the world had been like a wicked stepmother; never really wanting me to shine or to receive my inheritance. It was always taking from me and giving me nothing in return. Seemingly, it locked me away and made me struggle for everything. At that moment, my godmother became my fairy godmother. I couldn't believe it. I was beyond happy. No one had ever gifted me anything of that magnitude, and she didn't have to do it, but she did. On top of everything she had already done, Anna said she would get my nails and hair done. The love I felt that day was unreal. It wasn't because of the material things. I've never been materialistic. It was because I knew they felt like I deserved it. Anna always had me spoiled, along with my grandparents. I never beat them down if they couldn't do anything for me. I think that's why they didn't have a problem with telling me "yes" every time I'd ask for something. Anna met a guy who was just getting out of jail. His name was Jarvis. He had served about 10 years in prison. I'm not sure how long it was, but it was a long time. He joined Anna with spoiling me. He paid for a lot of my things for prom, as well. They bought me a clutch, my jewelry and everything I needed for prom. Landon bought my corsage. It had real flowers. He wore a white tuxedo with a champagne colored vest. My grandfather let us take his new Yukon Denali to prom. Everything was beautiful.

We took lots of pictures, and we went eat to Chili's before prom. I never felt that beautiful in my life. After getting glammed up and ready to go, it hit me like a ton of bricks. My mom couldn't see me in this moment. She had been gone for 2 years at that time and I really missed her. She wasn't able to see me make my debut to world. She wasn't able to see me go to homecoming and win Winter Formal Queen. She wasn't able to help me get ready for prom. So many of my friends' moms were gifting them pearls or other little tokens of love that was passed down from generation to generation. I wanted those moments with my mom. I didn't let that stop me from having fun though. I bottled up those emotions and let the good times roll. Everything went well until my boyfriend decided to get a hotel room after prom. All the seniors spent the night at the

Holiday Inn. My grandparents called my phone several times, but I didn't answer it. My grandfather had a pick-up truck, and he was determined to find me because I wasn't answering the phone. Whelp, he must've gone to every hotel until he saw his truck. All I heard was the loud engine from his truck and him blowing the horn like crazy outside. He blew the horn for about an hour straight, Ya'll. I couldn't believe he was embarrassing me like that. After he saw I wasn't coming out, he finally left. I lied and told my grandmother that my friend Ashton and I were at the hotel and that's where the prom after party was. I was lying and fussing at the same time. I was fussing about my grandfather embarrassing me in front of my friends. That's what you're supposed to do after prom. You supposed to stay out until the next morning. My grandmother looked at me and said, "Girl, if you don't get out of my face. We are not worried about you". I knew that was my cue to get out of her room with that fake buckin' before she put me in a head lock. My grandfather rolled his eyes at me that whole day. I didn't care though. I had a great night. I was in love and everything was turning around for me.

I got accepted to the college I wanted to attend, also. Like I said, I made it by the skin of my teeth. Out of everybody that was leaving to pursue their careers, I was going to miss Cliff the most. He was going to Hollywood to pursue his acting career. His videos "Da Berry" landed him on the news. He made our school famous. The class of 2007 was the best class ever. I know the other classes won't agree, but our basketball team won the state championship that year for the first time ever. As graduation approached, I was faced with a difficult decision. My grandmother asked if I wanted to give my dad a ticket to the graduation ceremony. I wanted to. It seemed like it didn't matter to me if he was a part of my life or not. I just loved him. At that point, I'd never really gotten to know him, but I always felt connected to him, especially with this big nose of mine. It looks identical to his. I hated my nose. I went to see him and gave him a ticket. He hugged me and said I'm coming baby girl. He definitely showed up. My dad, godmother, grandparents, aunt, uncle and Anna were all in attendance. Anna and my godmother took me to Ruby Tuesday's to eat after graduation. My boyfriend Landon came to eat with us too. My senior book was filled with signatures, positive messages, and senior pictures from all my friends and classmates. My senior pictures were taken by the photographer that took pictures for the local newspaper. He was my grandmother's friend. My grandmother always had friends that came through for her when needed. Every birthday and Valentine's Day, she would send us balloons and a bear to school. Mr. Paul's flower shop would deliver it. She had good friends that knew she was raising her daughter's children, so they helped her out a lot.

I couldn't believe I was walking across that stage. I finally made it across the finish line. I really didn't think I would. I thought I was going to have a baby by now or be a high school dropout, but I defeated the odds. My mom got someone in jail to draw me one of those fancy jail house cards. It said congratulations on graduating high school. My grandmother was still feeling bad, and she still wasn't working as much as she used to because of her appointments. I had a graduation party paid for by Anna and Jarvis. They brought sacks of crawfish. He got me a DJ. And, he told me that no matter what, he'd always be there for me. He meant that and he was there every time we needed him. They rented tables and chairs. All of my friends came out and we had a blast.

Now I'm getting ready for the real world. I was getting ready for college. I went to orientation with my friend Mitchell, but after paying for my dorm room and going through the financial aid process, I decided against it. It hurt me to leave my grandmother to take care of my siblings on her own. I stayed home and opted out of going to college to pursue a major in pre-law and a minor in mass communications. I always wanted to be an attorney and a journalist. Those were my passions. I wanted that so bad. I wanted to be able to put the bad guys away and to work for the newspaper or a big magazine company. My boyfriend encouraged me to go, but I knew I would be a financial strain on my grandparents with my mom still being in prison. I just wanted to help her. My youngest sister's dad, his girlfriend and her children moved across the street from us to help out. My baby sister had a learning disorder and my grandmother thought it was due to my mom being on drugs. I don't know if that was the reason, but I knew my grandmother always tried to justify her behavior. She wasn't hard on her like she was on us. I knew it was because of her illness, so I didn't trip on her about it. I took the big sister role more seriously, once I realized she was falling behind.

Chapter 11

Allison was doing great in school; better than I ever did. She always made good grades. Sunny was in 1st grade. I went to every field trip she had. I went to every meeting to see what we could do to improve her learning experience. I attended parent teacher conferences and even substituted in her class whenever they needed me. One day, someone from the school called and told me Sunny wasn't feeling well. I asked if I could come get her. I called my grandmother at work to see if it was ok for me to go get her. She told me it was ok. I put on my shoes and walked across the street to the school. When we got home, her dad saw us walk in the house. He came marching in behind us. I'm turning the combination on my padlock again. He's the same man who was ok with us living at a motel where prostitutes hung out and not having food, other than cereal and water. I always felt like he never cared about my mom's children. He only wanted to be with my mom by himself, without us. He took her to Baton Rouge without us too. I still showed him respect when he moved nearby to be closer to my sister and to take some of the weight off my grandmother. He even lived with us for a while when his girlfriend left him. He came storming in behind us and asked why she was checked out. I told him about the call from school and that my grandmother told me to go get her. He went on and on ranting about him being her father, that we needed to consult him before going get her and that we had no right. He said he was going to deal with my grandmother when she got home. My grandmother had to travel so far to see her doctor the day before. She still had the strength to get up for work the next day. I told him that he wasn't going to address her at all being that she's the sole provider for my sister. He didn't help my grandmother take care of my sister financially at all. He barely spent time with her. He was just there. I asked him to get out of our house. He lived across the street. I told him to leave, go to his house, and I'll inform my grandmother that he was upset about her being checked out. He called me every curse word in the book, so I slammed the door as he walked out. He busted through the door, pulled me outside and started fighting me. He fought me like I was a man. He pushed me, body slammed me, cursed me out and pulled my hair. My feelings about him not caring for us were definitely accurate. It was too easy for him to attack me. He just needed a reason, and he created one. My aunt was living with them across the street. She was in one of her moods. She was against us too because she didn't even bulge while he was fighting me. I think her and my grandmother may have gotten into an argument over something. When she's mad with one person, she takes it out on everybody. His girlfriend was yelling for him to stop, but he continued. He finally stopped when he heard people yelling from their cars. I ran in the house and grabbed the phone to call my grandmother. She told me not to call the police. She would deal with him when she got home. I wanted to call the police so bad. My head and back were killing me. He pulled some of my hair out from the front of my head. I had scratches on my face.

I called my cousin Anna. She heard me crying and her and her boyfriend showed up on 2 wheels. I called Landon too. He was furious! He had just gotten off of work and he flew straight to our house. As soon as he jumped out of his car, he went across the street to fight my sister's dad. They started fighting and my boyfriend whipped his butt. I was standing there yelling, "Do to him what you did to me". My aunt was buckin' on my boyfriend. She wanted to jump in until she saw Anna's boyfriend get out of the car. He had a reputation for knocking people out. She knew better than to jump in that. She piped down and backed away from the fight. If she was the way she used to be, she would've tried to fight both of them. She was losing so much weight from whatever drugs she was using at the time. When people think you don't have anybody coming behind you, they'll treat you any kind of way. That hurt me to my core. I had already opted out of going to college to stay home to help and now I'm still having to fight with people I don't want to fight with. My boyfriend beat him like he owed him money. My boyfriend was in the beginning stages of growing his dreads. My sister's dad was pulling his hair like he was fighting a woman. He was yelling for his girlfriend to call the police. She ran in the house to call the police. My cousin's boyfriend grabbed my boyfriend and told him to leave because she was calling the police on him. We jumped in the car and left. We went meet Landon's mom whom I loved dearly. We created such an amazing relationship throughout the course of my relationship with her son. She had such a good heart, but she had a lot of haters because of her beauty. You would never believe that she gave birth to 5 boys. She looked like she was 17 years old, right along with me. She was in her early 40's and was fine as wine. We didn't give the police a chance to come arrest him. His mom advised him to go to the police station and tell them what happened. We did. They didn't arrest him, but they gave him papers to go to court. The police told us that my aunt signed a statement against my boyfriend in defense of my sister's dad. My grandmother did not need any of that stress, but she called me and whispered to me on the phone. She said, "That's what he gets". She was happy that my boyfriend defended me. Even though she loved my sister's dad, she loved me more. My grandfather was mad too. He didn't play behind me either.

After all that drama was over, I spent the next few days at Landon's house. I thought I had a virus because I kept throwing up, the entire time I was there. Come to find out, I didn't have a virus at all. My insurance had dropped me, so I wasn't able to get birth control anymore. As a result, I was pregnant. I had just completed enrollment for the community college. I came up with a plan. I was going to take online courses to become a paralegal. Then, I would work my way to the top, once my grandmother was feeling better. I don't know how I let myself get in this situation. I was beyond scared to tell my grandmother that I was pregnant. She was going to kill me. I was going to pull up my big girl panties and do what I had to do. My boyfriend was supportive just like he was with everything else. He was so excited about the baby. I finally told my grandmother. She didn't react as I thought she would. She hugged me and said she already knew. She said she dreamt about fish. I found out I was having a boy. My grandmother started buying all kinds of clothes for him. My aunt and I made amends. She started buying things for the baby and being nice to me.

I lived with my boyfriend for the most part, but things started falling apart when he started cheating on me. I felt him changing. He wasn't being mean to me or anything, but he was always gone and that wasn't like him. Insecurity hit me like a brick in the face. Again, I was crumbling the leaves in my hands and watching the wind take it away. I had so much more than that on my plate. At my next doctor's appointment, I was told that my baby's heart was the size of a football. They didn't know if I would make it through the 8-month mark. His spinal cord wasn't connecting to his brain either. I immediately began to cry.

Why me? The doctor told me if my baby did make it, he would have so many medical issues and he would be in constant pain. Landon's mom came with me to that appointment. She held my hand tight and rubbed my back. She was very supportive. This was too much for me to take in, at the moment. I called my grandmother after we left the doctor's office. She told me not to worry about it. She said we would all pull through and help with him. Even if he had special needs, he would still be loved and taken care of. I called Landon to tell him about our baby's condition. He promised that we would get through it. He said he was going to help me and that we would get him the best wheelchair money could buy. He said he was going to make sure his shoe game was nice. I laughed and cried at the same time. That made me hopeful that everything would work out.

I began preparing my heart and mind to raise a special needs child. I did so much research. My mom called that week, also. I told her what was going on, and she prayed for me and my baby over the phone. I cried and cried. I felt like it was my fault because I had been stressing so much. All of my check-ups were going great. His condition wasn't getting any better, but I was hopeful that everything would work in our favor. I'm turning the combination on my padlock again. I was seeing a specialist and my regular OBGYN. They were constantly running tests and doing ultrasounds. Then, during a doctor's appointment, the technician was performing my ultrasound and she had a nervous look on her face. She looked worried. I asked her what was wrong. She told me she couldn't hear my baby's heartbeat and his heart wasn't moving on the screen. The ultrasound technician called the doctor in and he tried to find the heartbeat. He gently pushed on my stomach with his fingertips. He wiped my stomach off and put more gel on it. He looked for himself and the heartbeat machine was silent. The technician's eyes got teary and the doctor told me how sorry he was. He told me that I needed to go to the hospital immediately because my baby had passed away. I had gone to that appointment by myself. I had to call Landon to come pick me up. He rushed from work to bring me to the hospital. I tried to be brave in that moment, but it just felt so unreal. For 7 months, he became a part of me. His heart pounded on the inside of me. His legs and arms moved on the inside of me. We were connected and now I'm prevented from seeing the seed that was planted on the inside of me grow into a strong man. This was a different type of pain. This was a hurt that I wouldn't wish on anyone. When I got to the hospital, they explained to me what was about to happen. I had to be induced. They gave me a pill to take. In my mind, I was thinking that maybe they'd made a mistake. I wanted to convince myself that when he was delivered, his eyes would be opened, he would be crying, and his heart would be beating again. Landon called our families to tell them what happened. They started showing up to the hospital. Within a few hours, my beautiful son was delivered. I named him Elijah. Everyone held him, but I couldn't. I didn't have the strength to hold him. I looked at him while he was in everyone's arms and I felt so empty inside. I couldn't believe I wouldn't be able to bathe him, comb his hair or rock him to sleep. I felt so helpless. He was supposed to be here with me.

Finally, they were getting ready to take him out of the room. The nurse came closer to the bed to allow me to see him. Once she left the room, Anna rubbed my hand and told me it was ok to cry. I had gotten so used to throwing things in my closet and putting the padlock on it, that I didn't want to cry. I wanted to be strong, but I couldn't. I let it out. I cried like I've never cried before. The lady came in to discuss the funeral arrangements. I had to have a funeral for him because I was so far along. Within a few days, we had a funeral for him, and his obituary was in the newspaper. I just couldn't believe that I was burying my baby. His little coffin was so small. Everyone was so hurt. Landon and his mom both broke down at the funeral. We were all so excited about this pregnancy. My grandfather and other family members cooked for everyone after the funeral. I laid in the bed for days just drowning in sorrow. I tried my hardest to shake back, but the flatter my stomach got, the more reality sunk in.

On my 21st birthday and after 5 long years, my mom was released from prison. She came home with a new boyfriend. He was a Bishop she'd met while doing ministry work in prison. When she got home, we thought she was going to stay home with us, but she told us she was going live with her new boyfriend. Well, he was her husband because they had gotten married the day before my birthday. Allison and I were furious. We begged her to stay with us, but he kept yelling her name and telling her to get in the car. My grandfather wanted to fight him. My grandmother grabbed us by the hands and told us not to worry about it. She said she would always be our momma. Allison cried and screamed for my mom to stay with us. She left with him anyway. A week later, I was sleeping on the sofa and I had a dream that my grandmother died. I woke up sweating. Next thing you know, I heard my grandfather screaming my grandmother's name. I walked in their room and she was unresponsive. I grabbed my cell phone and called the paramedics. We tried to give her CPR. I was so nervous. My heart was beating so fast. I kept checking her pulse, but there was none. The paramedics arrived. They tried everything they could to get a response, but she didn't respond. They put her on a stretcher, put her in the truck and escorted her to the hospital. My baby sister was sleeping in the bed with her when all of this happened. I grabbed her and dressed both of us, so we could go to the hospital. When we got there, they told us that it was nothing more they could do. She had gone home to glory. My aunt punched the hospital glass door. All you could hear throughout the hospital hallways was screaming and crying. My queen, my mentor, the woman who considered me to be her own had left us. She would give you the shirt off her back. I always wanted to be like her. Her heart was like no other. She invested in me. Anything I wanted to do, she was there. The last conversation we had was me begging her to go to the hospital, as I held her head up so she could drink some water. She told me it was nothing they could do, and that hospice was about to start coming in. I even called my cousin Anna, who was in nursing school at the time, to talk her into going to the hospital. Then later that night, she left me. I made sure her funeral was the way she would've wanted it. Watching that casket go into the ground, made it so real. I missed her laugh and her scent. I missed her cursing me out in her proper voice, and I was going to miss our movie nights. My angel got her wings. She made it over. I was heartbroken, but I knew she wasn't in pain anymore.

Chapter 12

A lot transpired after my grandmother passed away. There were a lot of bad things and a lot of good things. My mom's ex-husband, the man that molested me, is now serving 2 consecutive life sentences because he decided to harm another beautiful soul. My mom went to college and rekindled her relationship with all of her children. She was able to regain custody of her younger children. She and her husband started a church and a group home. The group home served to help people get off of drugs and to get their lives back. She graduated from college, and they purchased a home. My sister, Allison, had her first baby at the age of 16. She was a fighter. She went to nursing assistant school and pushed her way through. My grandfather still has me spoiled, of course. He means so much to me. He could've left after my grandmother died, but he still treats me like his daughter. My aunt took her life back from the enemy. Sometimes, you have to move away and start from scratch. She's married now, and she's very active in her community. It was declared that she had a mental disorder and wouldn't be able to work a regular job.

Now, she keeps a job or two, and she's usually the manager on each one. It was her choice to stop receiving assistance. She wanted to work for what she wanted. My uncle has a green thumb. He's currently growing his own vegetable garden and taking care of his family. He's pushed his way through his adversities, as well.

I have 4 beautiful children now. I call them the "Wolfpack". I have the pleasure of being the mommy of 2 boys and 2 girls. They are little scholars who love the Lord. They can recite scriptures and every book of the Bible. I would have to write another book to explain what took place between me and their fathers, but it wasn't anything I hadn't gone through before. The difference this time is that my beautiful seeds were produced through it all. I'm currently the host of my own internet talk show called "Tea Tuesday". T-E-A stands for "Teaching, Encouraging, and Achieving". I'm also the founder of an organization called SHE, which stands for "Saving, Healing and Empowering". I'd consider myself a community activist in the town we reside in. I was determined to become the person I needed when I was growing up. All of my life, I was in a tunnel getting comfortable being in the dark. I got comfortable with people walking all over me. I got comfortable being laughed at and bullied. I thought I deserved everything I was receiving. Things began to change drastically when I realized how precious my life is to myself and the people around me.

Picking out my grandmother's casket and getting her clothes ready for the funeral did something to me. She lived her life. She took care of so many people. The scary part was that I'd died, also. I was breathing, but I wasn't alive. My closet was piling up. It was busting at the seams. I'd lost my son. I'd lost my grandmother. I'd lost my childhood. I got tired of losing. I got tired of filling my voids with temporary fixes. I had enough of being a zombie. I was done being a floor mat for people. My closet was so full that everything I'd stuffed in it started to leak out at a more rapid pace. It started to smell. I had to do this for me. I had to get up from under that tree. The leaves served their purpose, but I wasn't serving mine. I had to stand in front of the door of my closet and turn the combination to unlock the padlock. I had to open the closet and face the ugly truth. I was determined in my mind that I wanted more. My story isn't unique. So many women have and still are experiencing abuse, abandonment and neglect. We go through the fire, but I made up my mind that I was going to come out without the smell of smoke.

I began to tell myself that I was beautiful. Because of that, I started to feel beautiful. I started going to church. My grandmother would try to get me to go in the past, but I was too tired to go. I remember Angel praying with me before and after dance team practice, my first-grade teacher who was trying to break generational curses off of me and my best friend Cliff for accepting me for who I was and encouraging me to be who I was meant to be. I remember my godmother and my cousin Anna who nurtured my mind and who were the perfect display of dignity and strength and

Mr. Walters for planting seeds of greatness inside of me. In all my seasons, there were people that God put in place to give me a pat on the back and to encourage me to finish the race. I was going through some unspeakable things. I decided to open the door to my closet. I started getting rid of all the things that no longer served me. I didn't need those things in my life anymore. I had to tell myself the opposite of what the enemy was trying to make me believe. I was forced to forgive all the people who were not mature enough to handle me properly. They didn't know what I meant to God. I had to forgive myself for believing that I was the one to blame for things that were out of my control. I had to forgive myself for doing things that were beneath who I'm destined to be. I forgave myself for settling.

My mom came home and introduced me to a Man named Jesus. I knew of Him, but I didn't have a relationship with Him. Once I developed a relationship with Him, I ran out of that tunnel and I didn't look back. I kept chasing after Him, and I'm still chasing after Him. He began to fill every void I had or that I thought I had. He was there all along. I tried it my own way, and I failed miserably at it. I tried it the way worldly people try it and that didn't work. My freedom arrived when I lifted my hands. I surrendered to Him. I lifted my hands like a little girl would lift their hands to a father. I gave Him permission to invade my life. I needed him to empty everything inside of me that was not of Him and fill me with a fire that hasn't burned out since I surrendered. I surrendered my will for His will for my life.

He began to tell me how much I was really worth. He gave me beauty for my ashes. I went from being bullied and called ugly from people of all ages, to having strangers smile at me and consult me for advice. The same people who criticized me are now complimenting me. I went from having friends drag me through the mud and tell all my business when they were mad at me, to making divine connections. I was so used to being a people pleaser, and I always needed people around to make me feel like I was somebody. Now, I'd consider myself a popular loner. People follow me, Ya'll. They want to hear what I have to say. They want me to pray for them. That dirty little project girl is trying to make a major impact on the world.

My freedom arrived when I began to tell myself the truth. I stopped defending my dysfunction. I stopped being a victim. I became an overcomer, a survivor. I picked up my crown and became the queen I was created to be. I remember feeling filthy and God ministered to my soul. When Jesus turned water into wine, He used jars they would ceremonially use to wash feet. He told the servants to fill them with water and bring them to the king. By the time they got to the king, the water was turned into the finest wine he'd ever had. If you could imagine, that had to be dirty jars of water, but from the time they left Jesus and made it to the king, it was wine. I walked with my dirty jars of water, and when I made it out of that tunnel, I turned into the best wine the world has ever had. I see people with my same story who have committed suicide or are on drugs.

That alone makes me thankful that I was able to come out of that darkness. I know the feeling though. They are only trying to relieve themselves from the pain. I'm sure the thoughts of what they've been through are tormenting them. That could've been me. I could've lost my mind. I could've thrown in the towel, but I pressed my way through the crowd. I pressed my way through the hurt and the pain. I pressed my way through the blood, sweat and tears. Nothing or no one could fix my issues, but God.

I didn't realize that I wasn't as healed as I thought I was until I opened my closet. I had to sort everything out. Throw some stuff away that I had outgrown. There were some things I was still holding on to. In order for me to be a better mother, a better friend and a better person, I had to burn up everything that was hindering me from being the best version of myself. I set fire to that closet. I went into isolation with just myself and God. The definition of healing is "the process of making or becoming sound or healthy again". I was sick. I was all over the place. I needed to be healed. It's a process. It doesn't happen overnight. There is no quick fix. You will still get tested, but the difference between being healed and unhealed is your RESPONSE. Your faith allows you to rest during a storm. I stopped operating out of my wounds. I stopped responding from my emotions. Instead, I now operate in love. Just imagine the relief you feel after carrying a bunch of bricks and finally putting them down. That's how I felt once I gave God everything that was in my hands. A weight was lifted off of me. I was free! I no longer sit under trees and pick up leaves to crumble. I no longer wish to be the leaves so that the wind would take me away. Now, I want to be the whole tree. Jeremiah 17:8 says, "For he shall be as a tree planted by the waters, and that spreadeth out her roots by the river, and shall not see when heat cometh, but her leaf shall be green; and shall not be careful in the year of drought, neither shall cease from yielding fruit." Every time I see a tree, I want to dance under them. I'd kick the dried-up leaves on the ground because just like that tree, my new leaves had come in. I turned my pain into purpose. Everything I produced from the inside of me was a result of my tests. Even though the seasons continued to change, I remained planted. Goodness and mercy have been my bodyguards. His glory has rested in my soul. I was broken, but His grace saved my life. I could've lost my mind, but He kept me. I could've been dead, but He kept me. It was Him keeping my head above the water all along.

So now, every morning, I start the day off by speaking things into the atmosphere. I've learned that I have the power and authority to shift my atmosphere, so that my atmosphere can't shift me! I declare: No weapon formed against me shall prosper. The right doors are opening for me. The right people are hearing about me. God, keep my heart pure and my hands clean. Thank you for keeping me in my right mind. I repent for all my sins; sins known and unknown. Prepare my mind for all the amazing things You have for me. Bless me God, so that I can be a blessing to others. I pray for new territory, new levels, new dimensions and provision for the vision for everyone that I'm connected to. Laziness and procrastination cannot be with me today, but determination and favor will be my companions! In Jesus name, Amen!

I don't care what you've gone through. Open your mouth and begin to declare greatness over your life. You have the power to turn that thing around, if you really want to and trust that it can be turned around. There is nothing my God cannot do. There is nothing too big for Him. Those mountains might look big, but our God is bigger. Just stretch your hands out, call His name, and He'll come see about you no matter where you are. You're never too dirty for Him to clean you up. I've unlocked and cleaned out my closet. So, now you know that you can too.

Made in the USA
Lexington, KY
11 September 2019